P9-CNH-849

DOVER · THRIFT · EDITIONS

Selected Poems

WALT WHITMAN

DOVER PUBLICATIONS, INC.
New York

DOVER THRIFT EDITIONS

EDITOR: STANLEY APPELBAUM

Copyright © 1991 by Dover Publications, Inc.
All rights reserved under Pan American and International Copyright Conventions

This new anthology, first published by Dover Publications, Inc., in 1991, contains poems reprinted from a standard edition of *Leaves of Grass*. See the new Note, facing, for further bibliographic data. The alphabetical lists were prepared specially for the present anthology.

Manufactured in the United States of America
Dover Publications, Inc.
31 East 2nd Street
Mineola, N.Y. 11501

Library of Congress Cataloging-in-Publication Data

Whitman, Walt, 1819–1892.
[Poems. Selections]
Selected poems / Walt Whitman.
p.   cm. — (Dover thrift editions)
"Contains poems reprinted from a standard edition of
Leaves of grass"—T.p. verso.
Includes index.
ISBN 0-486-26878-0 (pbk.)
I. Title.   II. Series.
PS3204   1991
811'.3—dc20   91-12447
CIP

Note

THE AMERICAN POET and essayist Walt Whitman (1819–1892) created an extremely personal and innovative form of blank verse, in which the long, spacious lines reflected the breadth of his universal vision and the untamed expanses of the young nation he celebrated. But the form was not the only startling and prophetic aspect of his poems; there was also the grass-roots democratic foundation of his thought, the glorification of the common laboring man in town and country all over the world, the great emphasis on woman as a fellow toiler and companion, and (a shock to many of Whitman's contemporaries) an unblinkered acknowledgment of the body and its sexual needs. The poems, composed over many decades, are also a record of such historic events as the Civil War, the death of Lincoln and the opening of the Suez Canal.

Whitman included virtually all his verse—constantly adding, revising and reorganizing material—in successive editions of *Leaves of Grass*, from the first (1855) through the "Deathbed Edition" (1891–92); posthumous poems were added in the 1897 edition. The text of the 24 representative and highly regarded poems chosen for the present anthology is that of the 1891–92 edition. There are two dates at the end of each poem; the year given on the left is the one in which that particular poem was composed or first published; the year on the right is that of its final revision and inclusion in *Leaves of Grass*.

Contents

The section titles refer to the sections into which Whitman divided *Leaves of Grass*, the constantly expanding volume in which he included virtually all his poetry. The poems whose titles begin at the left margin are not included in sections. The entire sequence here follows that in *Leaves of Grass*.

I Hear America Singing

I hear America singing, the varied carols I hear,
Those of mechanics, each one singing his as it should be blithe and
    strong,
The carpenter singing his as he measures his plank or beam,
The mason singing his as he makes ready for work, or leaves off
    work,
The boatman singing what belongs to him in his boat, the deck-hand
    singing on the steamboat deck,
The shoemaker singing as he sits on his bench, the hatter singing as
    he stands,
The wood-cutter's song, the ploughboy's on his way in the morning,
    or at noon intermission or at sundown,
The delicious singing of the mother, or of the young wife at work, or
    of the girl sewing or washing,
Each singing what belongs to him or her and to none else,
The day what belongs to the day—at night the party of young
    fellows, robust, friendly,
Singing with open mouths their strong melodious songs.

1860   1867

Starting from Paumanok

1

Starting from fish-shape Paumanok where I was born,
Well-begotten, and rais'd by a perfect mother,
After roaming many lands, lover of populous pavements,
Dweller in Mannahatta my city, or on southern savannas,
Or a soldier camp'd or carrying my knapsack and gun, or a miner in
    California,
Or rude in my home in Dakota's woods, my diet meat, my drink from
    the spring,
Or withdrawn to muse and meditate in some deep recess,
Far from the clank of crowds intervals passing rapt and happy,

1

Aware of the fresh free giver the flowing Missouri, aware of mighty
    Niagara,
Aware of the buffalo herds grazing the plains, the hirsute and strong-
    breasted bull,
Of earth, rocks, Fifth-month flowers experienced, stars, rain, snow,
    my amaze,
Having studied the mocking-bird's tones and the flight of the
    mountain-hawk,
And heard at dawn the unrivall'd one, the hermit thrush from the
    swamp-cedars,
Solitary, singing in the West, I strike up for a New World.

2

Victory, union, faith, identity, time,
The indissoluble compacts, riches, mystery,
Eternal progress, the kosmos, and the modern reports.

This then is life,
Here is what has come to the surface after so many throes and
    convulsions.

How curious! how real!
Underfoot the divine soil, overhead the sun.

See revolving the globe,
The ancestor-continents away group'd together,
The present and future continents north and south, with the isthmus
    between.

See, vast trackless spaces,
As in a dream they change, they swiftly fill,
Countless masses debouch upon them,
They are now cover'd with the foremost people, arts, institutions,
    known.

See, projected through time,
For me an audience interminable.
With firm and regular step they wend, they never stop,
Successions of men, Americanos, a hundred millions,
One generation playing its part and passing on,
Another generation playing its part and passing on in its turn,
With faces turn'd sideways or backward towards me to listen,
With eyes retrospective towards me.

3

Americanos! conquerors! marches humanitarian!
Foremost! century marches! Libertad! masses!
For you a programme of chants.

Chants of the prairies,
Chants of the long-running Mississippi, and down to the Mexican
    sea,
Chants of Ohio, Indiana, Illinois, Iowa, Wisconsin and Minnesota,
Chants going forth from the centre from Kansas, and thence equi-
    distant,
Shooting in pulses of fire ceaseless to vivify all.

4

Take my leaves America, take them South and take them North,
Make welcome for them everywhere, for they are your own off-
    spring,
Surround them East and West, for they would surround you,
And you precedents, connect lovingly with them, for they connect
    lovingly with you.

I conn'd old times,
I sat studying at the feet of the great masters,
Now if eligible O that the great masters might return and study me.

In the name of these States shall I scorn the antique?
Why these are the children of the antique to justify it.

5

Dead poets, philosophs, priests,
Martyrs, artists, inventors, governments long since,
Language-shapers on other shores,
Nations once powerful, now reduced, withdrawn, or desolate,
I dare not proceed till I respectfully credit what you have left wafted
    hither,
I have perused it, own it is admirable, (moving awhile among it,)
Think nothing can ever be greater, nothing can ever deserve more
    than it deserves,
Regarding it all intently a long while, then dismissing it,
I stand in my place with my own day here.

Here lands female and male,
Here the heir-ship and heiress-ship of the world, here the flame of
    materials,
Here spirituality the translatress, the openly-avow'd,
The ever-tending, the finalè of visible forms,
The satisfier, after due long-waiting now advancing,
Yes here comes my mistress the soul.

6

The soul,
Forever and forever—longer than soil is brown and solid—longer
    than water ebbs and flows.

I will make the poems of materials, for I think they are to be the most
    spiritual poems,
And I will make the poems of my body and of mortality,
For I think I shall then supply myself with the poems of my soul and
    of immortality.

I will make a song for these States that no one State may under any
    circumstances be subjected to another State,
And I will make a song that there shall be comity by day and by night
    between all the States, and between any two of them,
And I will make a song for the ears of the President, full of weapons
    with menacing points,
And behind the weapons countless dissatisfied faces;
And a song make I of the One form'd out of all,
The fang'd and glittering One whose head is over all,
Resolute warlike One including and over all,
(However high the head of any else that head is over all.)

I will acknowledge contemporary lands,
I will trail the whole geography of the globe and salute courteously
    every city large and small,
And employments! I will put in my poems that with you is heroism
    upon land and sea,
And I will report all heroism from an American point of view.

I will sing the song of companionship,
I will show what alone must finally compact these,
I believe these are to found their own ideal of manly love, indicating
    it in me,
I will therefore let flame from me the burning fires that were threat-
    ening to consume me,

I will lift what has too long kept down those smouldering fires,
I will give them complete abandonment,
I will write the evangel-poem of comrades and of love,
For who but I should understand love with all its sorrow and joy?
And who but I should be the poet of comrades?

7

I am the credulous man of qualities, ages, races,
I advance from the people in their own spirit,
Here is what sings unrestricted faith.

Omnes! omnes! let others ignore what they may,
I make the poem of evil also, I commemorate that part also,
I am myself just as much evil as good, and my nation is—and I say
     there is in fact no evil,
(Or if there is I say it is just as important to you, to the land or to me,
     as any thing else.)

I too, following many and follow'd by many, inaugurate a religion, I
     descend into the arena,
(It may be I am destin'd to utter the loudest cries there, the winner's
     pealing shouts,
Who knows? they may rise from me yet, and soar above every thing.)

Each is not for its own sake,
I say the whole earth and all the stars in the sky are for religion's
     sake.
I say no man has ever yet been half devout enough,
None has ever yet adored or worship'd half enough,
None has begun to think how divine he himself is, and how certain
     the future is.

I say that the real and permanent grandeur of these States must be
     their religion,
Otherwise there is no real and permanent grandeur;
(Nor character nor life worthy the name without religion,
Nor land nor man or woman without religion.)

8

What are you doing young man?
Are you so earnest, so given up to literature, science, art, amours?
These ostensible realities, politics, points?
Your ambition or business whatever it may be?

It is well—against such I say not a word, I am their poet also,
But behold! such swiftly subside, burnt up for religion's sake,
For not all matter is fuel to heat, impalpable flame, the essential life
  of the earth,
Any more than such are to religion.

9

What do you seek so pensive and silent?
What do you need camerado?
Dear son do you think it is love?

Listen dear son—listen America, daughter or son,
It is a painful thing to love a man or woman to excess, and yet it
  satisfies, it is great,
But there is something else very great, it makes the whole coincide,
It, magnificent, beyond materials, with continuous hands sweeps
  and provides for all.

10

Know you, solely to drop in the earth the germs of a greater religion,
The following chants each for its kind I sing.
My comrade!
For you to share with me two greatnesses, and a third one rising
  inclusive and more resplendent,
The greatness of Love and Democracy, and the greatness of Religion.

Melange mine own, the unseen and the seen,
Mysterious ocean where the streams empty,
Prophetic spirit of material shifting and flickering around me,
Living beings, identities now doubtless near us in the air that we
  know not of,
Contact daily and hourly that will not release me,
These selecting, these in hints demanded of me.

Not he with a daily kiss onward from childhood kissing me,
Has winded and twisted around me that which holds me to him,
Any more than I am held to the heavens and all the spiritual world,
After what they have done to me, suggesting themes.

O such themes—equalities! O divine average!
Warblings under the sun, usher'd as now, or at noon, or setting,

Strains musical flowing through ages, now reaching hither,
I take to your reckless and composite chords, add to them, and
    cheerfully pass them forward.

11

As I have walk'd in Alabama my morning walk,
I have seen where the she-bird the mocking-bird sat on her nest in
    the briers hatching her brood.
I have seen the he-bird also,
I have paus'd to hear him near at hand inflating his throat and
    joyfully singing.

And while I paus'd it came to me that what he really sang for was not
    there only,
Nor for his mate nor himself only, nor all sent back by the echoes,
But subtle, clandestine, away beyond,
A charge transmitted and gift occult for those being born.

12

Democracy! near at hand to you a throat is now inflating itself and
    joyfully singing.

Ma femme! for the brood beyond us and of us,
For those who belong here and those to come,
I exultant to be ready for them will now shake out carols stronger and
    haughtier than have ever yet been heard upon earth.

I will make the songs of passion to give them their way,
And your songs outlaw'd offenders, for I scan you with kindred eyes,
    and carry you with me the same as any.

I will make the true poem of riches,
To earn for the body and the mind whatever adheres and goes forward
    and is not dropt by death;
I will effuse egotism and show it underlying all, and I will be the
    bard of personality,
And I will show of male and female that either is but the equal of the
    other,
And sexual organs and acts! do you concentrate in me, for I am
    determin'd to tell you with courageous clear voice to prove you
    illustrious,

And I will show that there is no imperfection in the present, and can
    be none in the future,
And I will show that whatever happens to anybody it may be turn'd to
    beautiful results,
And I will show that nothing can happen more beautiful than
    death,
And I will thread a thread through my poems that time and events
    are compact,
And that all the things of the universe are perfect miracles, each as
    profound as any.

I will not make poems with reference to parts,
But I will make poems, songs, thoughts, with reference to ensemble,
And I will not sing with reference to a day, but with reference to all
    days,
And I will not make a poem nor the least part of a poem but has
    reference to the soul,
Because having look'd at the objects of the universe, I find there is
    no one nor any particle of one but has reference to the soul.

13

Was somebody asking to see the soul?
See, your own shape and countenance, persons, substances, beasts,
    the trees, the running rivers, the rocks and sands.

All hold spiritual joys and afterwards loosen them;
How can the real body ever die and be buried?

Of your real body and any man's or woman's real body,
Item for item it will elude the hands of the corpse-cleaners and pass
    to fitting spheres,
Carrying what has accrued to it from the moment of birth to the
    moment of death.

Not the types set up by the printer return their impression, the
    meaning, the main concern,
Any more than a man's substance and life or a woman's substance
    and life return in the body and the soul,
Indifferently before death and after death.

Behold, the body includes and is the meaning, the main concern,
    and includes and is the soul;
Whoever you are, how superb and how divine is your body, or any
    part of it!

14

Whoever you are, to you endless announcements!

Daughter of the lands did you wait for your poet?
Did you wait for one with a flowing mouth and indicative hand?
Toward the male of the States, and toward the female of the States,
Exulting words, words to Democracy's lands.

Interlink'd, food-yielding lands!
Land of coal and iron! land of gold! land of cotton, sugar, rice!
Land of wheat, beef, pork! land of wool and hemp! land of the apple
     and the grape!
Land of the pastoral plains, the grass-fields of the world! land of
     those sweet-air'd interminable plateaus!
Land of the herd, the garden, the healthy house of adobie!
Lands where the north-west Columbia winds, and where the south-
     west Colorado winds!
Land of the eastern Chesapeake! land of the Delaware!
Land of Ontario, Erie, Huron, Michigan!
Land of the Old Thirteen! Massachusetts land! land of Vermont and
     Connecticut!
Land of the ocean shores! land of sierras and peaks!
Land of boatmen and sailors! fishermen's land!
Inextricable lands! the clutch'd together! the passionate ones!
The side by side! the elder and younger brothers! the bony-limb'd!
The great women's land! the feminine! the experienced sisters and
     the inexperienced sisters!
Far breath'd land! Arctic braced! Mexican breez'd! the diverse! the
     compact!
The Pennsylvanian! the Virginian! the double Carolinian!
O all and each well-loved by me! my intrepid nations! O I at any rate
     include you all with perfect love!
I cannot be discharged from you! not from one any sooner than
     another!
O death! O for all that, I am yet of you unseen this hour with
     irrepressible love,
Walking New England, a friend, a traveler,
Splashing my bare feet in the edge of the summer ripples on Pau-
     manok's sands,
Crossing the prairies, dwelling again in Chicago, dwelling in every
     town,
Observing shows, births, improvements, structures, arts,

Listening to orators and oratresses in public halls,
Of and through the States as during life, each man and woman my
neighbor,
The Louisianian, the Georgian, as near to me, and I as near to him
and her,
The Mississippian and Arkansian yet with me, and I yet with any of
them,
Yet upon the plains west of the spinal river, yet in my house of
adobie,
Yet returning eastward, yet in the Seaside State or in Maryland,
Yet Kanadian cheerily braving the winter, the snow and ice welcome
to me,
Yet a true son either of Maine or of the Granite State, or the
Narragansett Bay State, or the Empire State,
Yet sailing to other shores to annex the same, yet welcoming every
new brother,
Hereby applying these leaves to the new ones from the hour they
unite with the old ones,
Coming among the new ones myself to be their companion and
equal, coming personally to you now,
Enjoining you to acts, characters, spectacles, with me.

15

With me with firm holding, yet haste, haste on.

For your life adhere to me,
(I may have to be persuaded many times before I consent to give
myself really to you, but what of that?
Must not Nature be persuaded many times?)

No dainty dolce affettuoso I,
Bearded, sun-burnt, gray-neck'd, forbidding, I have arrived,
To be wrestled with as I pass for the solid prizes of the universe,
For such I afford whoever can persevere to win them.

16

On my way a moment I pause,
Here for you! and here for America!
Still the present I raise aloft, still the future of the States I harbinge
glad and sublime,
And for the past I pronounce what the air holds of the red aborigines.

The red aborigines,
Leaving natural breaths, sounds of rain and winds, calls as of birds
 and animals in the woods, syllabled, to us for names,
Okonee, Koosa, Ottawa, Monongahela, Sauk, Natchez, Chatta-
 hoochee, Kaqueta, Oronoco,
Wabash, Miami, Saginaw, Chippewa, Oshkosh, Walla-Walla,
Leaving such to the States they melt, they depart, charging the water
 and the land with names.

17

Expanding and swift, henceforth,
Elements, breeds, adjustments, turbulent, quick and audacious,
A world primal again, vistas of glory incessant and branching,
A new race dominating previous ones and grander far, with new
 contests,
New politics, new literatures and religions, new inventions and
 arts.

These, my voice announcing—I will sleep no more but arise,
You oceans that have been calm within me! how I feel you, fathom-
 less, stirring, preparing unprecedented waves and storms.

18

See, steamers steaming through my poems,
See, in my poems immigrants continually coming and landing,
See, in arriere, the wigwam, the trail, the hunter's hut, the flatboat,
 the maize-leaf, the claim, the rude fence, and the backwoods
 village,
See, on the one side the Western Sea and on the other the Eastern
 Sea, how they advance and retreat upon my poems as upon
 their own shores,
See, pastures and forests in my poems—see, animals wild and
 tame—see, beyond the Kaw, countless herds of buffalo feeding
 on short curly grass,
See, in my poems, cities, solid, vast, inland, with paved streets,
 with iron and stone edifices, ceaseless vehicles, and com-
 merce,
See, the many-cylinder'd steam printing-press—see, the electric
 telegraph stretching across the continent,
See, through Atlantica's depths pulses American Europe reaching,
 pulses of Europe duly return'd,

See, the strong and quick locomotive as it departs, panting, blowing
the steam-whistle,
See, ploughmen ploughing farms—see, miners digging mines—
see, the numberless factories,
See, mechanics busy at their benches with tools—see from among
them superior judges, philosophs, Presidents, emerge, drest in
working dresses,
See, lounging through the shops and fields of the States, me well-
belov'd, close-held by day and night,
Hear the loud echoes of my songs there—read the hints come at
last.

19

O camerado close! O you and me at last, and us two only.
O a word to clear one's path ahead endlessly!
O something ecstatic and undemonstrable! O music wild!
O now I triumph—and you shall also;
O hand in hand—O wholesome pleasure—O one more desirer and
lover!
O to haste firm holding—to haste, haste on with me.
1860   1881

I Sing the Body Electric

1

I sing the body electric,
The armies of those I love engirth me and I engirth them,
They will not let me off till I go with them, respond to them,
And discorrupt them, and charge them full with the charge of the
soul.

Was it doubted that those who corrupt their own bodies conceal
themselves?
And if those who defile the living are as bad as they who defile the
dead?
And if the body does not do fully as much as the soul?
And if the body were not the soul, what is the soul?

2

The love of the body of man or woman balks account, the body itself
    balks account,
That of the male is perfect, and that of the female is perfect.

The expression of the face balks account,
But the expression of a well-made man appears not only in his face,
It is in his limbs and joints also, it is curiously in the joints of his
    hips and wrists,
It is in his walk, the carriage of his neck, the flex of his waist and
    knees, dress does not hide him,
The strong sweet quality he has strikes through the cotton and broad-
    cloth,
To see him pass conveys as much as the best poem, perhaps more,
You linger to see his back, and the back of his neck and shoulder-
    side.

The sprawl and fulness of babes, the bosoms and heads of women,
    the folds of their dress, their style as we pass in the street, the
    contour of their shape downwards,
The swimmer naked in the swimming-bath, seen as he swims
    through the transparent green-shine, or lies with his face up
    and rolls silently to and fro in the heave of the water,
The bending forward and backward of rowers in row-boats, the
    horseman in his saddle,
Girls, mothers, house-keepers, in all their performances,
The group of laborers seated at noon-time with their open dinner
    kettles, and their wives waiting,
The female soothing a child, the farmer's daughter in the garden or
    cow-yard,
The young fellow hoeing corn, the sleigh-driver driving his six
    horses through the crowd,
The wrestle of wrestlers, two apprentice-boys, quite grown, lusty,
    good-natured, native-born, out on the vacant lot at sundown
    after work,
The coats and caps thrown down, the embrace of love and re-
    sistance,
The upper-hold and under-hold, the hair rumpled over and blinding
    the eyes;
The march of firemen in their own costumes, the play of masculine
    muscle through clean-setting trowsers and waist-straps,

The slow return from the fire, the pause when the bell strikes
    suddenly again, and the listening on the alert,
The natural, perfect, varied attitudes, the bent head, the curv'd
    neck and the counting;
Such-like I love—I loosen myself, pass freely, am at the mother's
    breast with the little child,
Swim with the swimmers, wrestle with wrestlers, march in line with
    the firemen, and pause, listen, count.

3

I knew a man, a common farmer, the father of five sons,
And in them the fathers of sons, and in them the fathers of
    sons.

This man was of wonderful vigor, calmness, beauty of person,
The shape of his head, the pale yellow and white of his hair and
    beard, the immeasurable meaning of his black eyes, the rich-
    ness and breadth of his manners,
These I used to go and visit him to see, he was wise also,
He was six feet tall, he was over eighty years old, his sons were
    massive, clean, bearded, tan-faced, handsome,
They and his daughters loved him, all who saw him loved him,
They did not love him by allowance, they loved him with personal
    love,
He drank water only, the blood show'd like scarlet through the clear-
    brown skin of his face,
He was a frequent gunner and fisher, he sail'd his boat himself, he
    had a fine one presented to him by a ship-joiner, he had
    fowling-pieces presented to him by men that loved him,
When he went with his five sons and many grand-sons to hunt or fish,
    you would pick him out as the most beautiful and vigorous of
    the gang,
You would wish long and long to be with him, you would wish to sit
    by him in the boat that you and he might touch each other.

4

I have perceiv'd that to be with those I like is enough,
To stop in company with the rest at evening is enough,
To be surrounded by beautiful, curious, breathing, laughing flesh is
    enough,

To pass among them or touch any one, or rest my arm ever so lightly
  round his or her neck for a moment, what is this then?
I do not ask any more delight, I swim in it as in a sea.

There is something in staying close to men and women and looking
  on them, and in the contact and odor of them, that pleases the
  soul well,
All things please the soul, but these please the soul well.

5

This is the female form,
A divine nimbus exhales from it from head to foot,
It attracts with fierce undeniable attraction,
I am drawn by its breath as if I were no more than a helpless vapor,
  all falls aside but myself and it,
Books, art, religion, time, the visible and solid earth, and what was
  expected of heaven or fear'd of hell, are now consumed,
Mad filaments, ungovernable shoots play out of it, the response
  likewise ungovernable,
Hair, bosom, hips, bend of legs, negligent falling hands all diffused,
  mine too diffused,
Ebb stung by the flow and flow stung by the ebb, love-flesh swelling
  and deliciously aching,
Limitless limpid jets of love hot and enormous, quivering jelly of
  love, white-blow and delirious juice,
Bridegroom night of love working surely and softly into the prostrate
  dawn,
Undulating into the willing and yielding day,
Lost in the cleave of the clasping and sweet-flesh'd day.

This the nucleus—after the child is born of woman, man is born of
  woman,
This the bath of birth, this the merge of small and large, and the
  outlet again.

Be not ashamed women, your privilege encloses the rest, and is the
  exit of the rest,
You are the gates of the body, and you are the gates of the soul.

The female contains all qualities and tempers them,
She is in her place and moves with perfect balance,
She is all things duly veil'd, she is both passive and active,

She is to conceive daughters as well as sons, and sons as well as
    daughters.

As I see my soul reflected in Nature,
As I see through a mist, One with inexpressible completeness,
    sanity, beauty,
See the bent head and arms folded over the breast, the Female
    I see.

6

The male is not less the soul nor more, he too is in his place,
He too is all qualities, he is action and power,
The flush of the known universe is in him,
Scorn becomes him well, and appetite and defiance become him
    well,
The wildest largest passions, bliss that is utmost, sorrow that is
    utmost become him well, pride is for him,
The full-spread pride of man is calming and excellent to the
    soul,
Knowledge becomes him, he likes it always, he brings every thing to
    the test of himself,
Whatever the survey, whatever the sea and the sail he strikes sound-
    ings at last only here,
(Where else does he strike soundings except here?)

The man's body is sacred and the woman's body is sacred,
No matter who it is, it is sacred—is it the meanest one in the
    laborer's gang?
Is it one of the dull-faced immigrants just landed on the wharf?
Each belongs here or anywhere just as much as the well-off, just as
    much as you,
Each has his or her place in the procession.

(All is a procession,
The universe is a procession with measured and perfect motion.)

Do you know so much yourself that you call the meanest igno-
    rant?
Do you suppose you have a right to a good sight, and he or she has no
    right to a sight?
Do you think matter has cohered together from its diffuse float, and

the soil is on the surface, and water runs and vegetation sprouts,
For you only, and not for him and her?

7

A man's body at auction,
(For before the war I often go to the slave-mart and watch the sale,)
I help the auctioneer, the sloven does not half know his business.

Gentlemen look on this wonder,
Whatever the bids of the bidders they cannot be high enough for it,
For it the globe lay preparing quintillions of years without one animal or plant,
For it the revolving cycles truly and steadily roll'd.

In this head the all-baffling brain,
In it and below it the makings of heroes.

Examine these limbs, red, black, or white, they are cunning in tendon and nerve,
They shall be stript that you may see them.

Exquisite senses, life-lit eyes, pluck, volition,
Flakes of breast-muscle, pliant backbone and neck, flesh not flabby, good-sized arms and legs,
And wonders within there yet.

Within there runs blood,
The same old blood! the same red-running blood!
There swells and jets a heart, there all passions, desires, reachings, aspirations,
(Do you think they are not there because they are not express'd in parlors and lecture-rooms?)

This is not only one man, this the father of those who shall be fathers in their turns,
In him the start of populous states and rich republics,
Of him countless immortal lives with countless embodiments and enjoyments.

How do you know who shall come from the offspring of his offspring through the centuries?

(Who might you find you have come from yourself, if you could trace
back through the centuries?)

8

A woman's body at auction,
She too is not only herself, she is the teeming mother of mothers,
She is the bearer of them that shall grow and be mates to the
mothers.

Have you ever loved the body of a woman?
Have you ever loved the body of a man?
Do you not see that these are exactly the same to all in all nations
and times all over the earth?

If any thing is sacred the human body is sacred,
And the glory and sweat of a man is the token of manhood untainted,
And in man or woman a clean, strong, firm-fibred body, is more
beautiful than the most beautiful face.
Have you seen the fool that corrupted his own live body? or the fool
that corrupted her own live body?
For they do not conceal themselves, and cannot conceal them-
selves.

9

O my body! I dare not desert the likes of you in other men and
women, nor the likes of the parts of you,
I believe the likes of you are to stand or fall with the likes of the soul,
(and that they are the soul,)
I believe the likes of you shall stand or fall with my poems, and that
they are my poems,
Man's, woman's, child's, youth's, wife's, husband's, mother's, fa-
ther's, young man's, young woman's poems,
Head, neck, hair, ears, drop and tympan of the ears,
Eyes, eye-fringes, iris of the eye, eyebrows, and the waking or
sleeping of the lids,
Mouth, tongue, lips, teeth, roof of the mouth, jaws, and the jaw-
hinges,
Nose, nostrils of the nose, and the partition,
Cheeks, temples, forehead, chin, throat, back of the neck, neck-
slue,

Strong shoulders, manly beard, scapula, hind-shoulders, and the
   ample side-round of the chest,
Upper-arm, armpit, elbow-socket, lower-arm, arm-sinews, arm-
   bones,
Wrist and wrist-joints, hand, palm, knuckles, thumb, forefinger,
   finger-joints, finger-nails,
Broad breast-front, curling hair of the breast, breast-bone, breast-
   side,
Ribs, belly, backbone, joints of the backbone,
Hips, hip-sockets, hip-strength, inward and outward round, man-
   balls, man-root,
Strong set of thighs, well carrying the trunk above,
Leg-fibres, knee, knee-pan, upper-leg, under-leg,
Ankles, instep, foot-ball, toes, toe-joints, the heel;
All attitudes, all the shapeliness, all the belongings of my or your
   body or of any one's body, male or female,
The lung-sponges, the stomach-sac, the bowels sweet and clean,
The brain in its folds inside the skull-frame,
Sympathies, heart-valves, palate-valves, sexuality, maternity,
Womanhood and all that is a woman, and the man that comes from
   woman,
The womb, the teats, nipples, breast-milk, tears, laughter, weeping,
   love-looks, love-perturbations and risings,
The voice, articulation, language, whispering, shouting aloud,
Food, drink, pulse, digestion, sweat, sleep, walking, swimming,
Poise on the hips, leaping, reclining, embracing, arm-curving and
   tightening,
The continual changes of the flex of the mouth, and around the eyes,
The skin, the sunburnt shade, freckles, hair,
The curious sympathy one feels when feeling with the hand the
   naked meat of the body,
The circling rivers the breath, and breathing it in and out,
The beauty of the waist, and thence of the hips, and thence down-
   ward toward the knees,
The thin red jellies within you or within me, the bones and the
   marrow in the bones,
The exquisite realization of health;
O say these are not the parts and poems of the body only, but of the
   soul,
O say now these are the soul!

1855   1881

Once I Pass'd through a Populous City

Once I pass'd through a populous city imprinting my brain for future
    use with its shows, architecture, customs, traditions,
Yet now of all that city I remember only a woman I casually met there
    who detain'd me for love of me,
Day by day and night by night we were together—all else has long
    been forgotten by me,
I remember I say only that woman who passionately clung to me,
Again we wander, we love, we separate again,
Again she holds me by the hand, I must not go,
I see her close beside me with silent lips sad and tremulous.

1860   1867

Recorders Ages Hence

Recorders ages hence,
Come, I will take you down underneath this impassive exterior, I will
    tell you what to say of me,
Publish my name and hang up my picture as that of the tenderest
    lover,
The friend the lover's portrait, of whom his friend his lover was
    fondest,
Who was not proud of his songs, but of the measureless ocean of love
    within him, and freely pour'd it forth,
Who often walk'd lonesome walks thinking of his dear friends, his
    lovers,
Who pensive away from one he lov'd often lay sleepless and dissat-
    isfied at night,
Who knew too well the sick, sick dread lest the one he lov'd might
    secretly be indifferent to him,
Whose happiest days were far away through fields, in woods, on
    hills, he and another wandering hand in hand, they twain apart
    from other men,
Who oft as he saunter'd the streets curv'd with his arm the shoulder
    of his friend, while the arm of his friend rested upon him also.

1860   1867

I Hear It Was Charged against Me

I hear it was charged against me that I sought to destroy institutions,
But really I am neither for nor against institutions,
(What indeed have I in common with them? or what with the destruc-
    tion of them?)
Only I will establish in the Mannahatta and in every city of these
    States inland and seaboard,
And in the fields and woods, and above every keel little or large that
    dents the water,
Without edifices or rules or trustees or any argument,
The institution of the dear love of comrades.

1860   1867

Salut au Monde!

1

O take my hand Walt Whitman!
Such gliding wonders! such sights and sounds!
Such join'd unended links, each hook'd to the next,
Each answering all, each sharing the earth with all.

What widens within you Walt Whitman?
What waves and soils exuding?
What climes? what persons and cities are here?
Who are the infants, some playing, some slumbering?
Who are the girls? who are the married women?
Who are the groups of old men going slowly with their arms about
    each other's necks?
What rivers are these? what forests and fruits are these?
What are the mountains call'd that rise so high in the mists?
What myriads of dwellings are they fill'd with dwellers?

2

Within me latitude widens, longitude lengthens,
Asia, Africa, Europe, are to the east—America is provided for in
    the west,
Banding the bulge of the earth winds the hot equator,

Curiously north and south turn the axis-ends,
Within me is the longest day, the sun wheels in slanting rings, it does
    not set for months,
Stretch'd in due time within me the midnight sun just rises above the
    horizon and sinks again,
Within me zones, seas, cataracts, forests, volcanoes, groups,
Malaysia, Polynesia, and the great West Indian islands.

3

What do you hear Walt Whitman?

I hear the workman singing and the farmer's wife singing,
I hear in the distance the sounds of children and of animals early in
    the day,
I hear emulous shouts of Australians pursuing the wild horse,
I hear the Spanish dance with castanets in the chestnut shade, to the
    rebeck and guitar,
I hear continual echoes from the Thames,
I hear fierce French liberty songs,
I hear of the Italian boat-sculler the musical recitative of old
    poems,
I hear the locusts in Syria as they strike the grain and grass with the
    showers of their terrible clouds,
I hear the Coptic refrain toward sundown, pensively falling on the
    breast of the black venerable vast mother the Nile,
I hear the chirp of the Mexican muleteer, and the bells of the mule,
I hear the Arab muezzin calling from the top of the mosque,
I hear the Christian priests at the altars of their churches, I hear the
    responsive base and soprano,
I hear the cry of the Cossack, and the sailor's voice putting to sea at
    Okotsk,
I hear the wheeze of the slave-coffle as the slaves march on, as the
    husky gangs pass on by twos and threes, fasten'd together with
    wrist-chains and ankle-chains,
I hear the Hebrew reading his records and psalms,
I hear the rhythmic myths of the Greeks, and the strong legends of
    the Romans,
I hear the tale of the divine life and bloody death of the beautiful God
    the Christ,
I hear the Hindoo teaching his favorite pupil the loves, wars, adages,
    transmitted safely to this day from poets who wrote three thou-
    sand years ago.

4

What do you see Walt Whitman?
Who are they you salute, and that one after another salute you?

I see a great round wonder rolling through space,
I see diminute farms, hamlets, ruins, graveyards, jails, factories,
    palaces, hovels, huts of barbarians, tents of nomads upon the
    surface,
I see the shaded part on one side where the sleepers are sleeping,
    and the sunlit part on the other side,
I see the curious rapid change of the light and shade,
I see distant lands, as real and near to the inhabitants of them as my
    land is to me.

I see plenteous waters,
I see mountain peaks, I see the sierras of Andes where they range,
I see plainly the Himalayas, Chian Shahs, Altays, Ghauts,
I see the giant pinnacles of Elbruz, Kazbek, Bazardjusi,
I see the Styrian Alps, and the Karnac Alps,
I see the Pyrenees, Balks, Carpathians, and to the north the Dof-
    rafields, and off at sea mount Hecla,
I see Vesuvius and Etna, the mountains of the Moon, and the Red
    mountains of Madagascar,
I see the Lybian, Arabian, and Asiatic deserts,
I see huge dreadful Arctic and Antarctic icebergs,
I see the superior oceans and the interior ones, the Atlantic and
    Pacific, the sea of Mexico, the Brazilian sea, and the sea of
    Peru,
The waters of Hindustan, the China sea, and the gulf of Guinea,
The Japan waters, the beautiful bay of Nagasaki land-lock'd in its
    mountains,
The spread of the Baltic, Caspian, Bothnia, the British shores, and
    the bay of Biscay,
The clear-sunn'd Mediterranean, and from one to another of its
    islands,
The White sea, and the sea around Greenland.

I behold the mariners of the world,
Some are in storms, some in the night with the watch on the lookout,
Some drifting helplessly, some with contagious diseases.

I behold the sail and steamships of the world, some in clusters in
    port, some on their voyages,

Some double the cape of Storms, some cape Verde, others capes
    Guardafui, Bon, or Bajadore,
Others Dondra head, others pass the straits of Sunda, others cape
    Lopatka, others Behring's straits,
Others cape Horn, others sail the gulf of Mexico or along Cuba or
    Hayti, others Hudson's bay or Baffin's bay,
Others pass the straits of Dover, others enter the Wash, others the
    firth of Solway, others round cape Clear, others the Land's End,
Others traverse the Zuyder Zee or the Scheld,
Others as comers and goers at Gibraltar or the Dardanelles,
Others sternly push their way through the northern winter-packs,
Others descend or ascend the Obi or the Lena,
Others the Niger or the Congo, others the Indus, the Burampooter
    and Cambodia,
Others wait steam'd up ready to start in the ports of Australia,
Wait at Liverpool, Glasgow, Dublin, Marseilles, Lisbon, Naples,
    Hamburg, Bremen, Bordeaux, the Hague, Copenhagen,
Wait at Valparaiso, Rio Janeiro, Panama.

5

I see the tracks of the railroads of the earth,
I see them in Great Britain, I see them in Europe,
I see them in Asia and in Africa.

I see the electric telegraphs of the earth,
I see the filaments of the news of the wars, deaths, losses, gains,
    passions, of my race.

I see the long river-stripes of the earth,
I see the Amazon and the Paraguay,
I see the four great rivers of China, the Amour, the Yellow River, the
    Yiang-tse, and the Pearl,
I see where the Seine flows, and where the Danube, the Loire, the
    Rhone, and the Guadalquiver flow,
I see the windings of the Volga, the Dnieper, the Oder,
I see the Tuscan going down the Arno, and the Venetian along the Po,
I see the Greek seaman sailing out of Egina bay.

6

I see the sight of the old empire of Assyria, and that of Persia, and
    that of India,
I see the falling of the Ganges over the high rim of Saukara.

I see the place of the idea of the Deity incarnated by avatars in
    human forms,
I see the spots of the successions of priests on the earth, oracles,
    sacrificers, brahmins, sabians, llamas, monks, muftis, ex-
    horters,
I see where druids walk'd the groves of Mona, I see the mistletoe and
    vervain,
I see the temples of the deaths of the bodies of Gods, I see the old
    signifiers.

I see Christ eating the bread of his last supper in the midst of youths
    and old persons,
I see where the strong divine young man the Hercules toil'd faith-
    fully and long and then died,
I see the place of the innocent rich life and hapless fate of the
    beautiful nocturnal son, the full-limb'd Bacchus,
I see Kneph, blooming, drest in blue, with the crown of feathers on
    his head,
I see Hermes, unsuspected, dying, well-belov'd, saying to the peo-
    ple *Do not weep for me,*
This is not my true country, I have lived banish'd from my true country,
    I now go back there,
I return to the celestial sphere where every one goes in his turn.

7

I see the battle-fields of the earth, grass grows upon them and
    blossoms and corn,
I see the tracks of ancient and modern expeditions.
I see the nameless masonries, venerable messages of the unknown
    events, heroes, records of the earth.

I see the places of the sagas,
I see pine-trees and fir-trees torn by northern blasts,
I see granite bowlders and cliffs, I see green meadows and lakes,
I see the burial-cairns of Scandinavian warriors,
I see them raised high with stones by the marge of restless oceans,
    that the dead men's spirits when they wearied of their quiet
    graves might rise up through the mounds and gaze on the tossing
    billows, and be refresh'd by storms, immensity, liberty, action.

I see the steppes of Asia,
I see the tumuli of Mongolia, I see the tents of Kalmucks and
    Baskirs,

I see the nomadic tribes with herds of oxen and cows,
I see the table-lands notch'd with ravines, I see the jungles and
 deserts,
I see the camel, the wild steed, the bustard, the fat-tail'd sheep, the
 antelope, and the burrowing wolf.

I see the highlands of Abyssinia,
I see flocks of goats feeding, and see the fig-tree, tamarind, date,
And see fields of teff-wheat and places of verdure and gold.

I see the Brazilian vaquero,
I see the Bolivian ascending mount Sorata,
I see the Wacho crossing the plains, I see the incomparable rider of
 horses with his lasso on his arm,
I see over the pampas the pursuit of wild cattle for their hides.

8, [9]

I see the regions of snow and ice,
I see the sharp-eyed Samoiede and the Finn,
I see the seal-seeker in his boat poising his lance,
I see the Siberian on his slight-built sledge drawn by dogs,
I see the porpoise-hunters, I see the whale-crews of the south Pacific
 and the north Atlantic,
I see the cliffs, glaciers, torrents, valleys, of Switzerland—I mark
 the long winters and the isolation.

I see the cities of the earth and make myself at random a part of
 them,
I am a real Parisian,
I am a habitan of Vienna, St. Petersburg, Berlin, Constantinople,
I am of Adelaide, Sidney, Melbourne,
I am of London, Manchester, Bristol, Edinburgh, Limerick,
I am of Madrid, Cadiz, Barcelona, Oporto, Lyons, Brussels, Berne,
 Frankfort, Stuttgart, Turin, Florence,
I belong in Moscow, Cracow, Warsaw, or northward in Christiania or
 Stockholm, or in Siberian Irkutsk, or in some street in Iceland,
I descend upon all those cities, and rise from them again.

10

I see vapors exhaling from unexplored countries,
I see the savage types, the bow and arrow, the poison'd splint, the
 fetich, and the obi.

I see African and Asiatic towns,
I see Algiers, Tripoli, Derne, Mogadore, Timbuctoo, Monrovia,
I see the swarms of Pekin, Canton, Benares, Delhi, Calcutta, Tokio,
I see the Kruman in his hut, and the Dahoman and Ashanteeman in
    their huts,
I see the Turk smoking opium in Aleppo,
I see the picturesque crowds at the fairs of Khiva and those of Herat,
I see Teheran, I see Muscat and Medina and the intervening sands, I
    see the caravans toiling onward,
I see Egypt and the Egyptians, I see the pyramids and obelisks,
I look on chisell'd histories, records of conquering kings, dynasties,
    cut in slabs of sand-stone, or on granite-blocks,
I see at Memphis mummy-pits containing mummies embalm'd,
    swathed in linen-cloth, lying there many centuries,
I look on the fall'n Theban, the large-ball'd eyes, the side-drooping
    neck, the hands folded across the breast.

I see all the menials of the earth, laboring,
I see all the prisoners in the prisons,
I see the defective human bodies of the earth,
The blind, the deaf and dumb, idiots, hunchbacks, lunatics,
The pirates, thieves, betrayers, murderers, slave-makers of the
    earth,
The helpless infants, and the helpless old men and women.

I see male and female everywhere,
I see the serene brotherhood of philosophs,
I see the constructiveness of my race,
I see the results of the perseverance and industry of my race,
I see ranks, colors, barbarisms, civilizations, I go among them, I
    mix indiscriminately,
And I salute all the inhabitants of the earth.

11

You whoever you are!
You daughter or son of England!
You of the mighty Slavic tribes and empires! you Russ in Russia!
You dim-descended, black, divine-soul'd African, large, fine-
    headed, nobly-form'd, superbly destin'd, on equal terms
    with me!
You Norwegian! Swede! Dane! Icelander! you Prussian!
You Spaniard of Spain! you Portuguese!

You Frenchwoman and Frenchman of France!
You Belge! you liberty-lover of the Netherlands! (you stock whence I
    myself have descended;)
You sturdy Austrian! you Lombard! Hun! Bohemian! farmer of Sty-
    ria!
You neighbor of the Danube!
You working-man of the Rhine, the Elbe, or the Weser! you working-
    woman too!
You Sardinian! you Bavarian! Swabian! Saxon! Wallachian! Bulgar-
    ian!
You Roman! Neapolitan! you Greek!
You lithe matador in the arena at Seville!
You mountaineer living lawlessly on the Taurus or Caucasus!
You Bokh horse-herd watching your mares and stallions feeding!
You beautiful-bodied Persian at full speed in the saddle shooting
    arrows to the mark!
You Chinaman and Chinawoman of China! you Tartar of Tartary!
You women of the earth subordinated at your tasks!
You Jew journeying in your old age through every risk to stand once
    on Syrian ground!
You other Jews waiting in all lands for your Messiah!
You thoughtful Armenian pondering by some stream of the Eu-
    phrates! you peering amid the ruins of Nineveh! you ascending
    mount Ararat!
You foot-worn pilgrim welcoming the far-away sparkle of the min-
    arets of Mecca!
You sheiks along the stretch from Suez to Bab-el-mandeb ruling your
    families and tribes!
You olive-grower tending your fruit on fields of Nazareth, Damascus,
    or lake Tiberias!
You Thibet trader on the wide inland or bargaining in the shops of
    Lassa!
You Japanese man or woman! you liver in Madagascar, Ceylon,
    Sumatra, Borneo!
All you continentals of Asia, Africa, Europe, Australia, indifferent
    of place!
All you on the numberless islands of the archipelagoes of the
    sea!
And you of centuries hence when you listen to me!
And you each and everywhere whom I specify not, but include just
    the same!
Health to you! good will to you all, from me and America sent!

Each of us inevitable,
Each of us limitless—each of us with his or her right upon the
    earth,
Each of us allow'd the eternal purports of the earth,
Each of us here as divinely as any is here.

12

You Hottentot with clicking palate! you woolly-hair'd hordes!
You own'd persons dropping sweat-drops or blood-drops!
You human forms with the fathomless ever-impressive countenances
    of brutes!
You poor koboo whom the meanest of the rest look down upon for all
    your glimmering language and spirituality!
You dwarf'd Kamtschatkan, Greenlander, Lapp!
You Austral negro, naked, red, sooty, with protrusive lip, groveling,
    seeking your food!
You Caffre, Berber, Soudanese!
You haggard, uncouth, untutor'd Bedowee!
You plague-swarms in Madras, Nankin, Kaubul, Cairo!
You benighted roamer of Amazonia! you Patagonian! you Feejee-
    man!
I do not prefer others so very much before you either,
I do not say one word against you, away back there where you
    stand,
(You will come forward in due time to my side.)

13

My spirit has pass'd in compassion and determination around the
    whole earth,
I have look'd for equals and lovers and found them ready for me in all
    lands,
I think some divine rapport has equalized me with them.

You vapors, I think I have risen with you, moved away to distant
    continents, and fallen down there, for reasons,
I think I have blown with you you winds;
You waters I have finger'd every shore with you,
I have run through what any river or strait of the globe has run
    through,
I have taken my stand on the bases of peninsulas and on the high
    embedded rocks, to cry thence:

Salut au monde!
What cities the light or warmth penetrates I penetrate those cities
    myself,
All islands to which birds wing their way I wing my way myself.

Toward you all, in America's name,
I raise high the perpendicular hand, I make the signal,
To remain after me in sight forever,
For all the haunts and homes of men.

1856   1881

Song of the Open Road

1

Afoot and light-hearted I take to the open road,
Healthy, free, the world before me,
The long brown path before me leading wherever I choose.

Henceforth I ask not good-fortune, I myself am good-fortune,
Henceforth I whimper no more, postpone no more, need nothing,
Done with indoor complaints, libraries, querulous criticisms,
Strong and content I travel the open road.

The earth, that is sufficient,
I do not want the constellations any nearer,
I know they are very well where they are,
I know they suffice for those who belong to them.

(Still here I carry my old delicious burdens,
I carry them, men and women, I carry them with me wherever I go,
I swear it is impossible for me to get rid of them,
I am fill'd with them; and I will fill them in return.)

2

You road I enter upon and look around, I believe you are not all that
    is here,
I believe that much unseen is also here.

Here the profound lesson of reception, nor preference nor denial,
The black with his woolly head, the felon, the diseas'd, the illiterate
    person, are not denied;

The birth, the hasting after the physician, the beggar's tramp, the
    drunkard's stagger, the laughing party of mechanics,
The escaped youth, the rich person's carriage, the fop, the eloping
    couple,
The early market-man, the hearse, the moving of furniture into the
    town, the return back from the town,
They pass, I also pass, any thing passes, none can be interdicted,
None but are accepted, none but shall be dear to me.

3

You air that serves me with breath to speak!
You objects that call from diffusion my meanings and give them
    shape!
You light that wraps me and all things in delicate equable showers!
You paths worn in the irregular hollows by the roadsides!
I believe you are latent with unseen existences, you are so dear
    to me.

You flagg'd walks of the cities! you strong curbs at the edges!
You ferries! you planks and posts of wharves! you timber-lined sides!
    you distant ships!
You rows of houses! you window-pierc'd façades! you roofs!
You porches and entrances! you copings and iron guards!
You windows whose transparent shells might expose so much!
You doors and ascending steps! you arches!
You gray stones of interminable pavements! you trodden crossings!
From all that has touch'd you I believe you have imparted to your-
    selves, and now would impart the same secretly to me,
From the living and the dead you have peopled your impassive
    surfaces, and the spirits thereof would be evident and amicable
    with me.

4

The earth expanding right hand and left hand,
The picture alive, every part in its best light,
The music falling in where it is wanted, and stopping where it is not
    wanted,
The cheerful voice of the public road, the gay fresh sentiment of the
    road.

O highway I travel, do you say to me *Do not leave me?*
Do you say *Venture not—if you leave me you are lost?*

Do you say *I am already prepared, I am well-beaten and undenied,
adhere to me?*

O public road, I say back I am not afraid to leave you, yet I
love you,
You express me better than I can express myself,
You shall be more to me than my poem.

I think heroic deeds were all conceiv'd in the open air, and all free
poems also,
I think I could stop here myself and do miracles,
I think whatever I shall meet on the road I shall like, and whoever
beholds me shall like me,
I think whoever I see must be happy.

5

From this hour I ordain myself loos'd of limits and imaginary lines,
Going where I list, my own master total and absolute,
Listening to others, considering well what they say,
Pausing, searching, receiving, contemplating,
Gently, but with undeniable will, divesting myself of the holds that
would hold me.

I inhale great draughts of space,
The east and the west are mine, and the north and the south are
mine.

I am larger, better than I thought,
I did not know I held so much goodness.

All seems beautiful to me,
I can repeat over to men and women You have done such good to me I
would do the same to you,
I will recruit for myself and you as I go,
I will scatter myself among men and women as I go,
I will toss a new gladness and roughness among them,
Whoever denies me it shall not trouble me,
Whoever accepts me he or she shall be blessed and shall bless me.

6

Now if a thousand perfect men were to appear it would not
amaze me,

Now if a thousand beautiful forms of women appear'd it would not
    astonish me.

Now I see the secret of the making of the best persons,
It is to grow in the open air and to eat and sleep with the earth.

Here a great personal deed has room,
(Such a deed seizes upon the hearts of the whole race of men,
Its effusion of strength and will overwhelms law and mocks all
    authority and all argument against it.)

Here is the test of wisdom,
Wisdom is not finally tested in schools,
Wisdom cannot be pass'd from one having it to another not having it,
Wisdom is of the soul, is not susceptible of proof, is its own proof,
Applies to all stages and objects and qualities and is content,
Is the certainty of the reality and immortality of things, and the
    excellence of things;
Something there is in the float of the sight of things that provokes it
    out of the soul.

Now I re-examine philosophies and religions,
They may prove well in lecture-rooms, yet not prove at all under the
    spacious clouds and along the landscape and flowing currents.

Here is realization,
Here is a man tallied—he realizes here what he has in him,
The past, the future, majesty, love—if they are vacant of you, you
    are vacant of them.

Only the kernel of every object nourishes;
Where is he who tears off the husks for you and me?
Where is he that undoes stratagems and envelopes for you and me?

Here is adhesiveness, it is not previously fashion'd, it is apropos;
Do you know what it is as you pass to be loved by strangers?
Do you know the talk of those turning eye-balls?

7

Here is the efflux of the soul,
The efflux of the soul comes from within through embower'd gates,
    ever provoking questions,
These yearnings why are they? these thoughts in the darkness why
    are they?

Why are there men and women that while they are nigh me the
sunlight expands my blood?
Why when they leave me do my pennants of joy sink flat and lank?
Why are there trees I never walk under but large and melodious
thoughts descend upon me?
(I' think they hang there winter and summer on those trees and
always drop fruit as I pass;)
What is it I interchange so suddenly with strangers?
What with some driver as I ride on the seat by his side?
What with some fisherman drawing his seine by the shore as I walk
by and pause?
What gives me to be free to a woman's and man's good-will? what
gives them to be free to mine?

8

The efflux of the soul is happiness, here is happiness,
I think it pervades the open air, waiting at all times,
Now it flows unto us, we are rightly charged.

Here rises the fluid and attaching character,
The fluid and attaching character is the freshness and sweetness of
man and woman,
(The herbs of the morning sprout no fresher and sweeter every day
out of the roots of themselves, than it sprouts fresh and sweet
continually out of itself.)
Toward the fluid and attaching character exudes the sweat of the love
of young and old,
From it falls distill'd the charm that mocks beauty and attainments,
Toward it heaves the shuddering longing ache of contact.

9

Allons! whoever you are come travel with me!
Traveling with me you find what never tires.

The earth never tires,
The earth is rude, silent, incomprehensible at first, Nature is rude
and incomprehensible at first,
Be not discouraged, keep on, there are divine things well envelop'd,
I swear to you there are divine things more beautiful than words can
tell.

Allons! we must not stop here,
However sweet these laid-up stores, however convenient this dwell-
   ing we cannot remain here,
However shelter'd this port and however calm these waters we must
   not anchor here,
However welcome the hospitality that surrounds us we are permitted
   to receive it but a little while.

10

Allons! the inducements shall be greater,
We will sail pathless and wild seas,
We will go where winds blow, waves dash, and the Yankee clipper
   speeds by under full sail.

Allons! with power, liberty, the earth, the elements,
Health, defiance, gayety, self-esteem, curiosity;
Allons! from all formules!
From your formules, O bat-eyed and materialistic priests.

The stale cadaver blocks up the passage—the burial waits no
   longer.

Allons! yet take warning!
He traveling with me needs the best blood, thews, endurance,
None may come to the trial till he or she bring courage and health,
Come not here if you have already spent the best of yourself,
Only those may come who come in sweet and determin'd bodies,
No diseas'd person, no rum-drinker or venereal taint is permitted
   here.

(I and mine do not convince by arguments, similes, rhymes,
We convince by our presence.)

11

Listen! I will be honest with you,
I do not offer the old smooth prizes, but offer rough new prizes,
These are the days that must happen to you:
You shall not heap up what is call'd riches,
You shall scatter with lavish hand all that you earn or achieve,
You but arrive at the city to which you were destin'd, you hardly
   settle yourself to satisfaction before you are call'd by an irre-
   sistible call to depart,

You shall be treated to the ironical smiles and mockings of those who
  remain behind you,
What beckonings of love you receive you shall only answer with
  passionate kisses of parting,
You shall not allow the hold of those who spread their reach'd hands
  toward you.

12

Allons! after the great Companions, and to belong to them!
They too are on the road—they are the swift and majestic men—
  they are the greatest women,
Enjoyers of calms of seas and storms of seas,
Sailors of many a ship, walkers of many a mile of land,
Habituès of many distant countries, habituès of far-distant dwell-
  ings,
Trusters of men and women, observers of cities, solitary toilers,
Pausers and contemplators of tufts, blossoms, shells of the shore,
Dancers at wedding-dances, kissers of brides, tender helpers of
  children, bearers of children,
Soldiers of revolts, standers by gaping graves, lowerers-down of
  coffins,
Journeyers over consecutive seasons, over the years, the curious
  years each emerging from that which preceded it,
Journeyers as with companions, namely their own diverse phases,
Forth-steppers from the latent unrealized baby-days,
Journeyers gayly with their own youth, journeyers with their bearded
  and well-grain'd manhood,
Journeyers with their womanhood, ample, unsurpass'd, content,
Journeyers with their own sublime old age of manhood or woman-
  hood,
Old age, calm, expanded, broad with the haughty breadth of the
  universe,
Old age, flowing free with the delicious near-by freedom of death.

13

Allons! to that which is endless as it was beginningless,
To undergo much, tramps of days, rests of nights,
To merge all in the travel they tend to, and the days and nights they
  tend to,
Again to merge them in the start of superior journeys,
To see nothing anywhere but what you may reach it and pass it,

To conceive no time, however distant, but what you may reach it and
    pass it,
To look up or down no road but it stretches and waits for you,
    however long but it stretches and waits for you,
To see no being, not God's or any, but you also go thither,
To see no possession but you may possess it, enjoying all without
    labor or purchase, abstracting the feast yet not abstracting one
    particle of it,
To take the best of the farmer's farm and the rich man's elegant villa,
    and the chaste blessings of the well-married couple, and the
    fruits of orchards and flowers of gardens,
To take to your use out of the compact cities as you pass through,
To carry buildings and streets with you afterward wherever you go,
To gather the minds of men out of their brains as you encounter them,
    to gather the love out of their hearts,
To take your lovers on the road with you, for all that you leave them
    behind you,
To know the universe itself as a road, as many roads, as roads for
    traveling souls.

All parts away for the progress of souls,
All religion, all solid things, arts, governments—all that was or is
    apparent upon this globe or any globe, falls into niches and
    corners before the procession of souls along the grand roads of
    the universe.
Of the progress of souls of men and women along the grand roads of
    the universe, all other progress is the needed emblem and
    sustenance.

Forever alive, forever forward,
Stately, solemn, sad, withdrawn, baffled, mad, turbulent, feeble,
    dissatisfied,
Desperate, proud, fond, sick, accepted by men, rejected by men,
They go! they go! I know that they go, but I know not where they go,
But I know that they go toward the best—toward something great.

Whoever you are, come forth! or man or woman come forth!
You must not stay sleeping and dallying there in the house, though
    you built it, or though it has been built for you.

Out of the dark confinement! out from behind the screen!
It is useless to protest, I know all and expose it.

Behold through you as bad as the rest,
Through the laughter, dancing, dining, supping, of people,

Inside of dresses and ornaments, inside of those wash'd and trimm'd
faces,
Behold a secret silent loathing and despair.

No husband, no wife, no friend, trusted to hear the confession,
Another self, a duplicate of every one, skulking and hiding it goes,
Formless and wordless through the streets of the cities, polite and
bland in the parlors,
In the cars of railroads, in steamboats, in the public assembly,
Home to the houses of men and women, at the table, in the bedroom,
everywhere,
Smartly attired, countenance smiling, form upright, death under the
breast-bones, hell under the skull-bones,
Under the broadcloth and gloves, under the ribbons and artificial
flowers,
Keeping fair with the customs, speaking not a syllable of itself,
Speaking of any thing else but never of itself.

14

Allons! through struggles and wars!
The goal that was named cannot be countermanded.

Have the past struggles succeeded?
What has succeeded? yourself? your nation? Nature?
Now understand me well—it is provided in the essence of things
that from any fruition of success, no matter what, shall come
forth something to make a greater struggle necessary.

My call is the call of battle, I nourish active rebellion,
He going with me must go well arm'd,
He going with me goes often with spare diet, poverty, angry enemies,
desertions.

15

Allons! the road is before us!
It is safe—I have tried it—my own feet have tried it well—be not
detain'd!
Let the paper remain on the desk unwritten, and the book on the
shelf unopen'd!
Let the tools remain in the workshop! let the money remain unearn'd!
Let the school stand! mind not the cry of the teacher!

Let the preacher preach in his pulpit! let the lawyer plead in the
     court, and the judge expound the law.

Camerado, I give you my hand!
I give you my love more precise than money,
I give you myself before preaching or law;
Will you give me yourself? will you come travel with me?
Shall we stick by each other as long as we live?

1856   1881

Crossing Brooklyn Ferry

1

Flood-tide below me! I see you face to face!
Clouds of the west—sun there half an hour high—I see you also face
     to face.

Crowds of men and women attired in the usual costumes, how
     curious you are to me!
On the ferry-boats the hundreds and hundreds that cross, returning
     home, are more curious to me than you suppose,
And you that shall cross from shore to shore years hence are more to
     me, and more in my meditations, than you might suppose.

2

The impalpable sustenance of me from all things at all hours of
     the day,
The simple, compact, well-join'd scheme, myself disintegrated,
     every one disintegrated yet part of the scheme,
The similitudes of the past and those of the future,
The glories strung like beads on my smallest sights and hearings, on
     the walk in the street and the passage over the river,
The current rushing so swiftly and swimming with me far away,
The others that are to follow me, the ties between me and them,
The certainty of others, the life, love, sight, hearing of others.

Others will enter the gates of the ferry and cross from shore to shore,
Others will watch the run of the flood-tide,
Others will see the shipping of Manhattan north and west, and the
     heights of Brooklyn to the south and east,

Others will see the islands large and small;
Fifty years hence, others will see them as they cross, the sun half an
    hour high,
A hundred years hence, or ever so many hundred years hence,
    others will see them,
Will enjoy the sunset, the pouring-in of the flood-tide, the falling-
    back to the sea of the ebb-tide. *Positivity*

3

It avails not, time nor place—distance avails not, *Theme — find*
I am with you, you men and women of a generation, or ever so many *relat*
    generations hence, *theme*
Just as you feel when you look on the river and sky, so I felt,
Just as any of you is one of a living crowd, I was one of a
    crowd,
Just as you are refresh'd by the gladness of the river and the bright
    flow, I was refresh'd,
Just as you stand and lean on the rail, yet hurry with the swift
    current, I stood yet was hurried,
Just as you look on the numberless masts of ships and the thick-
    stemm'd pipes of steamboats, I look'd.

I too many and many a time cross'd the river of old, *Complexity*
Watched the Twelfth-month sea-gulls, saw them high in the air
    floating with motionless wings, oscillating their bodies,
Saw how the glistening yellow lit up parts of their bodies and left the
    rest in strong shadow,
Saw the slow-wheeling circles and the gradual edging toward the
    south,
Saw the reflection of the summer sky in the water,
Had my eyes dazzled by the shimmering track of beams,
Look'd at the fine centrifugal spokes of light round the shape of my
    head in the sunlit water,
Look'd on the haze on the hills southward and south-westward,
Look'd on the vapor as it flew in fleeces tinged with violet,
Look'd toward the lower bay to notice the vessels arriving,
Saw their approach, saw aboard those that were near me,
Saw the white sails of schooners and sloops, saw the ships at
    anchor,
The sailors at work in the rigging or out astride the spars,
The round masts, the swinging motion of the hulls, the slender
    serpentine pennants,

The large and small steamers in motion, the pilots in their pilot-
     houses,
The white wake left by the passage, the quick tremulous whirl of the
     wheels,
The flags of all nations, the falling of them at sunset,
The scallop-edged waves in the twilight, the ladled cups, the frolic-
     some crests and glistening,
The stretch afar growing dimmer and dimmer, the gray walls of the
     granite storehouses by the docks,
On the river the shadowy group, the big steam-tug closely flank'd on
     each side by the barges, the hay-boat, the belated lighter,
On the neighboring shore the fires from the foundry chimneys
     burning high and glaringly into the night,
Casting their flicker of black contrasted with wild red and yellow
     light over the tops of houses, and down into the clefts of streets.

4

These and all else were to me the same as they are to you,
I loved well those cities, loved well the stately and rapid river,
The men and women I saw were all near to me,
Others the same—others who look back on me because I look'd
     forward to them,
(The time will come, though I stop here to-day, and to-night.)

5

What is it then between us?
What is the count of the scores or hundreds of years between us?

Whatever it is, it avails not—distance avails not, and place
     avails not,
I too lived, Brooklyn of ample hills was mine,
I too walk'd the streets of Manhattan island, and bathed in the waters
     around it,
I too felt the curious abrupt questionings stir within me.
In the day among crowds of people sometimes they came upon me,
In my walks home late at night or as I lay in my bed they came
     upon me,
I too had been struck from the float forever held in solution,
I too had receiv'd identity by my body,
That I was I knew was of my body, and what I should be I knew I
     should be of my body.

6

It is not upon you alone the dark patches fall,
The dark threw its patches down upon me also,
The best I had done seem'd to me blank and suspicious,
My great thoughts as I supposed them, were they not in reality
    meagre?
Nor is it you alone who know what it is to be evil,
I am he who knew what it was to be evil,
I too knitted the old knot of contrariety,
Blabb'd, blush'd, resented, lied, stole, grudg'd,
Had guile, anger, lust, hot wishes I dared not speak,
Was wayward, vain, greedy, shallow, sly, cowardly, malignant,
The wolf, the snake, the hog, not wanting in me,
The cheating look, the frivolous word, the adulterous wish, not
    wanting,
Refusals, hates, postponements, meanness, laziness, none of these
    wanting,
Was one with the rest, the days and haps of the rest,
Was call'd by my nighest name by clear loud voices of young men as
    they saw me approaching or passing,
Felt their arms on my neck as I stood, or the negligent leaning of
    their flesh against me as I sat,
Saw many I loved in the street or ferry-boat or public assembly, yet
    never told them a word,
Lived the same life with the rest, the same old laughing, gnawing,
    sleeping,
Play'd the part that still looks back on the actor or actress,
The same old role, the role that is what we make it, as great as we
    like,
Or as small as we like, or both great and small.

7

Closer yet I approach you,
What thought you have of me now, I had as much of you—I laid in
    my stores in advance,
I consider'd long and seriously of you before you were born.

Who was to know what should come home to me?
Who knows but I am enjoying this?
Who knows, for all the distance, but I am as good as looking at you
    now, for all you cannot see me?

8

Ah, what can ever be more stately and admirable to me than mast-
hemm'd Manhattan?
River and sunset and scallop-edg'd waves of flood-tide?
The sea-gulls oscillating their bodies, the hay-boat in the twilight,
and the belated lighter?

What gods can exceed these that clasp me by the hand, and with
voices I love call me promptly and loudly by my nighest name
as I approach?

What is more subtle than this which ties me to the woman or man that
looks in my face?
Which fuses me into you now, and pours my meaning into you?

We understand then do we not?
What I promis'd without mentioning it, have you not accepted?
What the study could not teach—what the preaching could not
accomplish is accomplish'd, is it not?

9

Flow on, river! flow with the flood-tide, and ebb with the ebb-
tide!
Frolic on, crested and scallop-edg'd waves!
Gorgeous clouds of the sunset! drench with your splendor me, or the
men and women generations after me!
Cross from shore to shore, countless crowds of passengers!
Stand up, tall masts of Mannahatta! stand up, beautiful hills of
Brooklyn!
Throb, baffled and curious brain! throw out questions and answers!
Suspend here and everywhere, eternal float of solution!
Gaze, loving and thirsting eyes, in the house or street or public
assembly!
Sound out, voices of young men! loudly and musically call me by my
nighest name!
Live, old life! play the part that looks back on the actor or actress!
Play the old role, the role that is great or small according as one
makes it!
Consider, you who peruse me, whether I may not in unknown ways
be looking upon you;
Be firm, rail over the river, to support those who lean idly, yet haste
with the hasting current;

Fly on, sea-birds! fly sideways, or wheel in large circles high in
    the air;
Receive the summer sky, you water, and faithfully hold it till all
    downcast eyes have time to take it from you!
Diverge, fine spokes of light, from the shape of my head, or any one's
    head, in the sunlit water!
Come on, ships from the lower bay! pass up or down, white-sail'd
    schooners, sloops, lighters!
Flaunt away, flags of all nations! be duly lower'd at sunset!
Burn high your fires, foundry chimneys! cast black shadows at
    nightfall! cast red and yellow light over the tops of the houses!
Appearances, now or henceforth, indicate what you are,
You necessary film, continue to envelop the soul,
About my body for me, and your body for you, be hung our divinest
    aromas,
Thrive, cities—bring your freight, bring your shows, ample and
    sufficient rivers,
Expand, being than which none else is perhaps more spiritual,
Keep your places, objects than which none else is more lasting.

You have waited, you always wait, you dumb, beautiful ministers,
We receive you with free sense at last, and are insatiate hencefor-
    ward,
Not you any more shall be able to foil us, or withhold yourselves
    from us,
We use you, and do not cast you aside—we plant you permanently
    within us,
We fathom you not—we love you—there is perfection in you also,
You furnish your parts toward eternity,
Great or small, you furnish your parts toward the soul.

1856   1881

Song of the Broad-Axe

1

Weapon shapely, naked, wan,
Head from the mother's bowels drawn,
Wooded flesh and metal bone, limb only one and lip only one,
Gray-blue leaf by red-heat grown, helve produced from a little seed
    sown,

Resting the grass amid and upon,
To be lean'd and to lean on.

Strong shapes and attributes of strong shapes, masculine trades,
    sights and sounds,
Long varied train of an emblem, dabs of music,
Fingers of the organist skipping staccato over the keys of the great
    organ.

2

Welcome are all earth's lands, each for its kind,
Welcome are lands of pine and oak,
Welcome are lands of the lemon and fig,
Welcome are lands of gold,
Welcome are lands of wheat and maize, welcome those of the grape,
Welcome are lands of sugar and rice,
Welcome the cotton-lands, welcome those of the white potato and
    sweet potato,
Welcome are mountains, flats, sands, forests, prairies,
Welcome the rich borders of rivers, table-lands, openings,
Welcome the measureless grazing-lands, welcome the teeming soil
    of orchards, flax, honey, hemp;
Welcome just as much the other more hard-faced lands,
Lands rich as lands of gold or wheat and fruit lands,
Lands of mines, lands of the manly and rugged ores,
Lands of coal, copper, lead, tin, zinc,
Lands of iron—lands of the make of the axe.

3

The log at the wood-pile, the axe supported by it,
The sylvan hut, the vine over the doorway, the space clear'd for a
    garden,
The irregular tapping of rain down on the leaves after the storm is
    lull'd,
The wailing and moaning at intervals, the thought of the sea,
The thought of ships struck in the storm and put on their beam ends,
    and the cutting away of masts,
The sentiment of the huge timbers of old-fashion'd houses and
    barns,
The remember'd print or narrative, the voyage at a venture of men,
    families, goods,

The disembarkation, the founding of a new city,

The voyage of those who sought a New England and found it, the outset anywhere,

The settlements of the Arkansas, Colorado, Ottawa, Willamette,

The slow progress, the scant fare, the axe, rifle, saddle-bags;

The beauty of all adventurous and daring persons,

The beauty of wood-boys and wood-men with their clear untrimm'd faces,

The beauty of independence, departure, actions that rely on themselves,

The American contempt for statutes and ceremonies, the boundless impatience of restraint,

The loose drift of chàracter, the inkling through random types, the solidification;

The butcher in the slaughter-house, the hands aboard schooners and sloops, the raftsmen, the pioneer,

Lumbermen in their winter camp, daybreak in the woods, stripes of snow on the limbs of trees, the occasional snapping,

The glad clear sound of one's own voice, the merry song, the natural life of the woods, the strong day's work,

The blazing fire at night, the sweet taste of supper, the talk, the bed of hemlock-boughs and the bear-skin;

The house-builder at work in cities or anywhere,

The preparatory jointing, squaring, sawing, mortising,

The hoist-up of beams, the push of them in their places, laying them regular,

Setting the studs by their tenons in the mortises according as they were prepared,

The blows of mallets and hammers, the attitudes of the men, their curv'd limbs,

Bending, standing, astride the beams, driving in pins, holding on by posts and braces,

The hook'd arm over the plate, the other arm wielding the axe,

The floor-men forcing the planks close to be nail'd,

Their postures bringing their weapons downward on the bearers,

The echoes resounding through the vacant building;

The huge storehouse carried up in the city well under way,

The six framing-men, two in the middle and two at each end, carefully bearing on their shoulders a heavy stick for a cross-beam,

The crowded line of masons with trowels in their right hands rapidly laying the long side-wall, two hundred feet from front to rear,

The flexible rise and fall of backs, the continual click of the trowels
    striking the bricks,
The bricks one after another each laid so workmanlike in its place,
    and set with a knock of the trowel-handle,
The piles of materials, the mortar on the mortar-boards, and the
    steady replenishing by the hod-men;
Spar-makers in the spar-yard, the swarming row of well-grown ap-
    prentices,
The swing of their axes on the square-hew'd log shaping it toward the
    shape of a mast,
The brisk short crackle of the steel driven slantingly into the
    pine,
The butter-color'd chips flying off in great flakes and slivers,
The limber motion of brawny young arms and hips in easy costumes,
The constructor of wharves, bridges, piers, bulk-heads, floats, stays
    against the sea;
The city fireman, the fire that suddenly bursts forth in the close-
    pack'd square,
The arriving engines, the hoarse shouts, the nimble stepping and
    daring,
The strong command through the fire-trumpets, the falling in line,
    the rise and fall of the arms forcing the water,
The slender, spasmic, blue-white jets, the bringing to bear of the
    hooks and ladders and their execution,
The crash and cut away of connecting wood-work, or through floors if
    the fire smoulders under them,
The crowd with their lit faces watching, the glare and dense
    shadows;
The forger at his forge-furnace and the user of iron after him,
The maker of the axe large and small, and the welder and temperer,
The chooser breathing his breath on the cold steel and trying the
    edge with his thumb,
The one who clean-shapes the handle and sets it firmly in the socket;
The shadowy processions of the portraits of the past users also,
The primal patient mechanics, the architects and engineers,
The far-off Assyrian edifice and Mizra edifice,
The Roman lictors preceding the consuls,
The antique European warrior with his axe in combat,
The uplifted arm, the clatter of blows on the helmeted head,
The death-howl, the limpsy tumbling body, the rush of friend and foe
    thither,
The siege of revolted lieges determin'd for liberty,

The summons to surrender, the battering at castle gates, the truce
and parley,
The sack of an old city in its time,
The bursting in of mercenaries and bigots tumultuously and disor-
derly,
Roar, flames, blood, drunkenness, madness,
Goods freely rifled from houses and temples, screams of women in
the gripe of brigands,
Craft and thievery of camp-followers, men running, old persons
despairing,
The hell of war, the cruelties of creeds,
The list of all executive deeds and words just or unjust,
The power of personality just or unjust.

4

Muscle and pluck forever!
What invigorates life invigorates death,
And the dead advance as much as the living advance,
And the future is no more uncertain than the present,
For the roughness of the earth and of man encloses as much as the
delicatesse of the earth and of man,
And nothing endures but personal qualities.

What do you think endures?
Do you think a great city endures?
Or a teeming manufacturing state? or a prepared constitution? or the
best built steamships?
Or hotels of granite and iron? or any chef-d'œuvres of engineering,
forts, armaments?

Away! these are not to be cherish'd for themselves,
They fill their hour, the dancers dance, the musicians play for them,
The show passes, all does well enough of course,
All does very well till one flash of defiance.

A great city is that which has the greatest men and women,
If it be a few ragged huts it is still the greatest city in the whole
world.

5

The place where a great city stands is not the place of stretch'd
wharves, docks, manufactures, deposits of produce merely,

Nor the place of ceaseless salutes of new-comers or the anchor-lifters
    of the departing,
Nor the place of the tallest and costliest buildings or shops selling
    goods from the rest of the earth,
Nor the place of the best libraries and schools, nor the place where
    money is plentiest,
Nor the place of the most numerous population.

Where the city stands with the brawniest breed of orators and bards,
Where the city stands that is belov'd by these, and loves them in
    return and understands them,
Where no monuments exist to heroes but in the common words and
    deeds,
Where thrift is in its place, and prudence is in its place,
Where the men and women think lightly of the laws,
Where the slave ceases, and the master of slaves ceases,
Where the populace rise at once against the never-ending audacity
    of elected persons,
Where fierce men and women pour forth as the sea to the whistle of
    death pours its sweeping and unript waves,
Where outside authority enters always after the precedence of inside
    authority,
Where the citizen is always the head and ideal, and President,
    Mayor, Governor and what not, are agents for pay,
Where children are taught to be laws to themselves, and to depend
    on themselves,
Where equanimity is illustrated in affairs,
Where speculations on the soul are encouraged,
Where women walk in public processions in the streets the same as
    the men,
Where they enter the public assembly and take places the same as
    the men;
Where the city of the faithfulest friends stands,
Where the city of the cleanliness of the sexes stands,
Where the city of the healthiest fathers stands,
Where the city of the best-bodied mothers stands,
There the great city stands.

6

How beggarly appear arguments before a defiant deed!
How the floridness of the materials of cities shrivels before a man's or
    woman's look!

All waits or goes by default till a strong being appears;
A strong being is the proof of the race and of the ability of the
    universe,
When he or she appears materials are overaw'd,
The dispute on the soul stops,
The old customs and phrases are confronted, turn'd back, or laid
    away.

What is your money-making now? what can it do now?
What is your respectability now?
What are your theology, tuition, society, traditions, statute-books,
    now?
Where are your jibes of being now?
Where are your cavils about the soul now?

7

A sterile landscape covers the ore, there is as good as the best for all
    the forbidding appearance,
There is the mine, there are the miners,
The forge-furnace is there, the melt is accomplish'd, the hammers-
    men are at hand with their tongs and hammers,
What always served and always serves is at hand.

Than this nothing has better served, it has served all,
Served the fluent-tongued and subtle-sensed Greek, and long ere
    the Greek,
Served in building the buildings that last longer than any,
Served the Hebrew, the Persian, the most ancient Hindustanee,
Served the mound-raiser on the Mississippi, served those whose
    relics remain in Central America,
Served Albic temples in woods or on plains, with unhewn pillars and
    the druids,
Served the artificial clefts, vast, high, silent, on the snow-cover'd
    hills of Scandinavia,
Served those who time out of mind made on the granite walls rough
    sketches of the sun, moon, stars, ships, ocean waves,
Served the paths of the irruptions of the Goths, served the pastoral
    tribes and nomads,
Served the long distant Kelt, served the hardy pirates of the
    Baltic,
Served before any of those the venerable and harmless men of
    Ethiopia,

Served the making of helms for the galleys of pleasure and the
    making of those for war,
Served all great works on land and all great works on the sea,
For the mediæval ages and before the mediæval ages,
Served not the living only then as now, but served the dead.

8

I see the European headsman,
He stands mask'd, clothed in red, with huge legs and strong naked
    arms,
And leans on a ponderous axe.

(Whom have you slaughter'd lately European headsman?
Whose is that blood upon you so wet and sticky?)

I see the clear sunsets of the martyrs,
I see from the scaffolds the descending ghosts,
Ghosts of dead lords, uncrown'd ladies, impeach'd ministers, re-
    jected kings,
Rivals, traitors, poisoners, disgraced chieftains and the rest.

I see those who in any land have died for the good cause,
The seed is spare, nevertheless the crop shall never run out,
(Mind you O foreign kings, O priests, the crop shall never run out.)

I see the blood wash'd entirely away from the axe,
Both blade and helve are clean,
They spirt no more the blood of European nobles, they clasp no more
    the necks of queens.

I see the headsman withdraw and become useless,
I see the scaffold untrodden and mouldy, I see no longer any axe
    upon it,
I see the mighty and friendly emblem of the power of my own race,
    the newest, largest race.

9

(America! I do not vaunt my love for you,
I have what I have.)

The axe leaps!
The solid forest gives fluid utterances,
They tumble forth, they rise and form,
Hut, tent, landing, survey,

Flail, plough, pick, crowbar, spade,
Shingle, rail, prop, wainscot, jamb, lath, panel, gable,
Citadel, ceiling, saloon, academy, organ, exhibition-house, library,
Cornice, trellis, pilaster, balcony, window, turret, porch,
Hoe, rake, pitchfork, pencil, wagon, staff, saw, jack-plane, mallet,
    wedge, rounce,
Chair, tub, hoop, table, wicket, vane, sash, floor,
Work-box, chest, string'd instrument, boat, frame, and what not,
Capitols of States, and capitol of the nation of States,
Long stately rows in avenues, hospitals for orphans or for the poor or
    sick,
Manhattan steamboats and clippers taking the measure of all seas.

The shapes arise!
Shapes of the using of axes anyhow, and the users and all that
    neighbors them,
Cutters down of wood and haulers of it to the Penobscot or Kennebec,
Dwellers in cabins among the Californian mountains or by the little
    lakes, or on the Columbia,
Dwellers south on the banks of the Gila or Rio Grande, friendly
    gatherings, the characters and fun,
Dwellers along the St. Lawrence, or north in Kanada, or down by the
    Yellowstone, dwellers on coasts and off coasts,
Seal-fishers, whalers, arctic seamen breaking passages through the ice.

The shapes arise!
Shapes of factories, arsenals, foundries, markets,
Shapes of the two-threaded tracks of railroads,
Shapes of the sleepers of bridges, vast frameworks, girders, arches,
Shapes of the fleets of barges, tows, lake and canal craft, river craft,
Ship-yards and dry-docks along the Eastern and Western seas, and
    in many a bay and by-place,
The live-oak kelsons, the pine planks, the spars, the hackmatack-
    roots for knees,
The ships themselves on their ways, the tiers of scaffolds, the
    workmen busy outside and inside,
The tools lying around, the great auger and little auger, the adze,
    bolt, line, square, gouge, and bead-plane.

10

The shapes arise!
The shape measur'd, saw'd, jack'd, join'd, stain'd,

The coffin-shape for the dead to lie within in his shroud,
The shape got out in posts, in the bedstead posts, in the posts of the
    bride's bed,
The shape of the little trough, the shape of the rockers beneath, the
    shape of the babe's cradle,
The shape of the floor-planks, the floor-planks for dancer's feet,
The shape of the planks of the family home, the home of the friendly
    parents and children,
The shape of the roof of the home of the happy young man and
    woman, the roof over the well-married young man and woman,
The roof over the supper joyously cook'd by the chaste wife, and
    joyously eaten by the chaste husband, content after his day's
    work.

The shapes arise!
The shape of the prisoner's place in the court-room, and of him or
    her seated in the place.
The shape of the liquor-bar lean'd against by the young rum-drinker
    and the old rum-drinker,
The shape of the shamed and angry stairs trod by sneaking footsteps,
The shape of the sly settee, and the adulterous unwholesome couple,
The shape of the gambling-board with its devilish winnings and
    losings,
The shape of the step-ladder for the convicted and sentenced mur-
    derer, the murderer with haggard face and pinion'd arms,
The sheriff at hand with his deputies, the silent and white-lipp'd
    crowd, the dangling of the rope.

The shapes arise!
Shapes of doors giving many exits and entrances,
The door passing the dissever'd friend flush'd and in haste,
The door that admits good news and bad news,
The door whence the son left home confident and puff'd up,
The door he enter'd again from a long and scandalous absence,
    diseas'd, broken down, without innocence, without means.

11

Her shape arises,
She less guarded than ever, yet more guarded than ever,
The gross and soil'd she moves among do not make her gross and
    soil'd,

She knows the thoughts as she passes, nothing is conceal'd from her,
She is none the less considerate or friendly therefor,
She is the best belov'd, it is without exception, she has no reason to
    fear and she does not fear,
Oaths, quarrels, hiccupp'd songs, smutty expressions are idle to her
    as she passes,
She is silent, she is possess'd of herself, they do not offend her,
She receives them as the laws of Nature receive them, she is strong,
She too is a law of Nature—there is no law stronger than she is.

12

The main shapes arise!
Shapes of Democracy total, result of centuries,
Shapes ever projecting other shapes,
Shapes of turbulent manly cities,
Shapes of the friends and home-givers of the whole earth,
Shapes bracing the earth and braced with the whole earth.

1856   1881

Song of the Redwood-Tree

1

A California song,
A prophecy and indirection, a thought impalpable to breathe as air,
A chorus of dryads, fading, departing, or hamadryads departing,
A murmuring, fateful, giant voice, out of the earth and sky,
Voice of a mighty dying tree in the redwood forest dense.

Farewell my brethren,
Farewell O earth and sky, farewell ye neighboring waters,
My time has ended, my term has come.

Along the northern coast,
Just back from the rock-bound shore and the caves,
In the saline air from the sea in the Mendocino country,
With the surge for base and accompaniment low and hoarse,
With crackling blows of axes sounding musically driven by strong
    arms,

Riven deep by the sharp tongues of the axes, there in the redwood
    forest dense,
I heard the mighty tree its death-chant chanting.

The choppers heard not, the camp shanties echoed not,
The quick-ear'd teamsters and chain and jack-screw men heard not,
As the wood-spirits came from their haunts of a thousand years to
    join the refrain,
But in my soul I plainly heard.

Murmuring out of its myriad leaves,
Down from its lofty top rising two hundred feet high,
Out of its stalwart trunk and limbs, out of its foot-thick bark,
That chant of the seasons and time, chant not of the past only but the
    future.

You untold life of me,
And all you venerable and innocent joys,
Perennial hardy life of me with joys 'mid rain and many a summer sun,
And the white snows and night and the wild winds;
O the great patient rugged joys, my soul's strong joys unreck'd by man,
(For know I bear the soul befitting me, I too have consciousness,
    identity,
And all the rocks and mountains have, and all the earth,)
Joys of the life befitting me and brothers mine,
Our time, our term has come.

Nor yield we mournfully majestic brothers,
We who have grandly fill'd our time;
With Nature's calm content, with tacit huge delight,
We welcome what we wrought for through the past,
And leave the field for them.
For them predicted long,
For a superber race, they too to grandly fill their time,
For them we abdicate, in them ourselves ye forest kings!
In them these skies and airs, these mountain peaks, Shasta, Ne-
    vadas,
These huge precipitous cliffs, this amplitude, these valleys, far
    Yosemite,
To be in them absorb'd, assimilated.

Then to a loftier strain,
Still prouder, more ecstatic rose the chant,

As if the heirs, the deities of the West,
Joining with master-tongue bore part.

Not wan from Asia's fetiches,
Nor red from Europe's old dynastic slaughter-house,
(Area of murder-plots of thrones, with scent left yet of wars and
scaffolds everywhere,)
But come from Nature's long and harmless throes, peacefully builded
thence,
These virgin lands, lands of the Western shore,
To the new culminating man, to you, the empire new,
You promis'd long, we pledge, we dedicate.

You occult deep volitions,
You average spiritual manhood, purpose of all, pois'd on yourself,
giving not taking law,
You womanhood divine, mistress and source of all, whence life and
love and aught that comes from life and love,
You unseen moral essence of all the vast materials of America, (age
upon age working in death the same as life,)
You that, sometimes known, oftener unknown, really shape and mould
the New World, adjusting it to Time and Space,
You hidden national will lying in your abysms, conceal'd but ever
alert,
You past and present purposes tenaciously pursued, may-be uncon-
scious of yourselves,
Unswerv'd by all the passing errors, perturbations of the sur-
face;
You vital, universal, deathless germs, beneath all creeds, arts, stat-
utes, literatures,
Here build your homes for good, establish here, these areas entire,
lands of the Western shore,
We pledge, we dedicate to you.

For man of you, your characteristic race,
Here may he hardy, sweet, gigantic grow, here tower proportionate to
Nature,
Here climb the vast pure spaces unconfined, uncheck'd by wall or
roof,
Here laugh with storm or sun, here joy, here patiently inure,
Here heed himself, unfold himself, (not others' formulas heed,) here
fill his time,

To duly fall, to aid, unreck'd at last,
To disappear, to serve.

Thus on the northern coast,
In the echo of teamsters' calls and the clinking chains, and the music
  of choppers' axes,
The falling trunk and limbs, the crash, the muffled shriek, the groan,
Such words combined from the redwood-tree, as of voices ecstatic,
  ancient and rustling,
The century-lasting, unseen dryads, singing, withdrawing,
All their recesses of forests and mountains leaving,
From the Cascade range to the Wasatch, or Idaho far, or Utah,
To the deities of the modern henceforth yielding,
The chorus and indications, the vistas of coming humanity, the
  settlements, features all,
In the Mendocino woods I caught.

2

The flashing and golden pageant of California,
The sudden and gorgeous drama, the sunny and ample lands,
The long and varied stretch from Puget sound to Colorado south,
Lands bathed in sweeter, rarer, healthier air, valleys and mountain
  cliffs,
The fields of Nature long prepared and fallow, the silent, cyclic
  chemistry,
The slow and steady ages plodding, the unoccupied surface ripen-
  ing, the rich ores forming beneath;
At last the New arriving, assuming, taking possession,
A swarming and busy race settling and organizing everywhere,
Ships coming in from the whole round world, and going out to the
  whole world,
To India and China and Australia and the thousand island paradises
  of the Pacific,
Populous cities, the latest inventions, the steamers on the rivers, the
  railroads, with many a thrifty farm, with machinery,
And wood and wheat and the grape, and diggings of yellow gold.

3

But more in you than these, lands of the Western shore,
(These but the means, the implements, the standing-ground,)

I see in you, certain to come, the promise of thousands of years, till
    now deferr'd,
Promis'd to be fulfill'd, our common kind, the race.

The new society at last, proportionate to Nature,
In man of you, more than your mountain peaks or stalwart trees
    imperial,
In woman more, far more, than all your gold or vines, or even vital air.

Fresh come, to a new world indeed, yet long prepared,
I see the genius of the modern, child of the real and ideal,
Clearing the ground for broad humanity, the true America, heir of
    the past so grand,
To build a grander future.

1874   1881

A Song for Occupations

1

A song for occupations!
In the labor of engines and trades and the labor of fields I find the
    developments,
And find the eternal meanings.

Workmen and Workwomen!
Were all educations practical and ornamental well display'd out of
    me, what would it amount to?
Were I as the head teacher, charitable proprietor, wise statesman,
    what would it amount to?
Were I to you as the boss employing and paying you, would that
    satisfy you?

The learn'd, virtuous, benevolent, and the usual terms,
A man like me and never the usual terms.

Neither a servant nor a master I,
I take no sooner a large price than a small price, I will have my own
    whoever enjoys me,
I will be even with you and you shall be even with me.

If you stand at work in a shop I stand as nigh as the nighest in the
    same shop,

If you bestow gifts on your brother or dearest friend I demand as good
    as your brother or dearest friend,
If your lover, husband, wife, is welcome by day or night, I must be
    personally as welcome,
If you become degraded, criminal, ill, then I become so for your sake,
If you remember your foolish and outlaw'd deeds, do you think I
    cannot remember my own foolish and outlaw'd deeds?
If you carouse at the table I carouse at the opposite side of the table,
If you meet some stranger in the streets and love him or her, why I
    often meet strangers in the street and love them.

Why what have you thought of yourself?
Is it you then that thought yourself less?
Is it you that thought the President greater than you?
Or the rich better off than you? or the educated wiser than you?

(Because you are greasy or pimpled, or were once drunk, or a thief,
Or that you are diseas'd, or rheumatic, or a prostitute,
Or from frivolity or impotence, or that you are no scholar and never
    saw your name in print,
Do you give in that you are any less immortal?)

2

Souls of men and women! it is not you I call unseen, unheard,
    untouchable and untouching,
It is not you I go argue pro and con about, and to settle whether you
    are alive or no,
I own publicly who you are, if nobody else owns.

Grown, half-grown and babe, of this country and every country,
    indoors and out-doors, one just as much as the other, I see,
And all else behind or through them.

The wife, and she is not one jot less than the husband,
The daughter, and she is just as good as the son,
The mother, and she is every bit as much as the father.

Offspring of ignorant and poor, boys apprenticed to trades,
Young fellows working on farms and old fellows working on farms,
Sailor-men, merchant-men, coasters, immigrants,
All these I see, but nigher and farther the same I see,
None shall escape me and none shall wish to escape me.

I bring what you much need yet always have,
Not money, amours, dress, eating, erudition, but as good,

I send no agent or medium, offer no representative of value, but offer
the value itself.

There is something that comes to one now and perpetually,
It is not what is printed, preach'd, discussed, it eludes discussion
and print,
It is not to be put in a book, it is not in this book,
It is for you whoever you are, it is no farther from you than your
hearing and sight are from you,
It is hinted by nearest, commonest, readiest, it is ever provoked by
them.

You may read in many languages, yet read nothing about it,
You may read the President's message and read nothing about it
there,
Nothing in the reports from the State department or Treasury depart-
ment, or in the daily papers or weekly papers,
Or in the census or revenue returns, prices current, or any accounts
of stock.

3

The sun and stars that float in the open air,
The apple-shaped earth and we upon it, surely the drift of them is
something grand,
I do not know what it is except that it is grand, and that it is
happiness,
And that the enclosing purport of us here is not a speculation or bon-
mot or reconnoissance,
And that it is not something which by luck may turn out well for us,
and without luck must be a failure for us,
And not something which may yet be retracted in a certain contin-
gency.

The light and shade, the curious sense of body and identity, the
greed that with perfect complaisance devours all things,
The endless pride and outstretching of man, unspeakable joys and
sorrows,
The wonder every one sees in every one else he sees, and the
wonders that fill each minute of time forever,
What have you reckon'd them for, camerado?
Have you reckon'd them for your trade or farm-work? or for the
profits of your store?

Or to achieve yourself a position? or to fill a gentleman's leisure, or a lady's leisure?

Have you reckon'd that the landscape took substance and form that it might be painted in a picture?
Or men and women that they might be written of, and songs sung?
Or the attraction of gravity, and the great laws and harmonious combinations and the fluids of the air, as subjects for the savans?
Or the brown land and the blue sea for maps and charts?
Or the stars to be put in constellations and named fancy names?
Or that the growth of seeds is for agricultural tables, or agriculture itself?

Old institutions, these arts, libraries, legends, collections, and the practice handed along in manufactures, will we rate them so high?
Will we rate our cash and business high? I have no objection,
I rate them as high as the highest—then a child born of a woman and man I rate beyond all rate.

We thought our Union grand, and our Constitution grand,
I do not say they are not grand and good, for they are,
I am this day just as much in love with them as you,
Then I am in love with You, and with all my fellows upon the earth.

We consider bibles and religions divine—I do not say they are not divine,
I say they have all grown out of you, and may grow out of you still,
It is not they who give the life, it is you who give the life,
Leaves are not more shed from the trees, or trees from the earth, than they are shed out of you.

4

The sum of all known reverence I add up in you whoever you are,
The President is there in the White House for you, it is not you who are here for him,
The Secretaries act in their bureaus for you, not you here for them,
The Congress convenes every Twelfth-month for you,
Laws, courts, the forming of States, the charters of cities, the going and coming of commerce and mails, are all for you.

List close my scholars dear,
Doctrines, politics and civilization exurge from you,
Sculpture and monuments and any thing inscribed anywhere are tallied in you,

The gist of histories and statistics as far back as the records reach is
    in you this hour, and myths and tales the same,
If you were not breathing and walking here, where would they all be?
The most renown'd poems would be ashes, orations and plays would
    be vacuums.

All architecture is what you do to it when you look upon it,
(Did you think it was in the white or gray stone? or the lines of the
    arches and cornices?)
All music is what awakes from you when you are reminded by the
    instruments,
It is not the violins and the cornets, it is not the oboe nor the beating
    drums, nor the score of the baritone singer singing his sweet ro-
    manza, nor that of the men's chorus, nor that of the women's
    chorus,
It is nearer and farther than they.

5

Will the whole come back then?
Can each see signs of the best by a look in the looking-glass? is there
    nothing greater or more?
Does all sit there with you, with the mystic unseen soul?

Strange and hard that paradox true I give,
Objects gross and the unseen soul are one.

House-building, measuring, sawing the boards,
Blacksmithing, glass-blowing, nail-making, coopering, tin-roofing,
    shingle-dressing,
Ship-joining, dock-building, fish-curing, flagging of sidewalks by
    flaggers,
The pump, the pile-driver, the great derrick, the coal-kiln and
    brick-kiln,
Coal-mines and all that is down there, the lamps in the darkness,
    echoes, songs, what meditations, what vast native thoughts
    looking through smutch'd faces,
Iron-works, forge-fires in the mountains or by river-banks, men
    around feeling the melt with huge crowbars, lumps of ore, the
    due combining of ore, limestone, coal,
The blast-furnace and the puddling-furnace, the loup-lump at the
    bottom of the melt at last, the rolling-mill, the stumpy bars of
    pig-iron, the strong, clean-shaped T-rail for railroads,

Oil-works, silk-works, white-lead-works, the sugar-house, steam-
    saws, the great mills and factories,
Stone-cutting, shapely trimmings for façades or window or door-
    lintels, the mallet, the tooth-chisel, the jib to protect the
    thumb,
The calking-iron, the kettle of boiling vault-cement, and the fire
    under the kettle,
The cotton-bale, the stevedore's hook, the saw and buck of the
    sawyer, the mould of the moulder, the working-knife of the
    butcher, the ice-saw, and all the work with ice,
The work and tools of the rigger, grappler, sail-maker, block-maker,
Goods of gutta-percha, papier-maché, colors, brushes, brush-
    making, glazier's implements,
The veneer and glue-pot, the confectioner's ornaments, the decanter
    and glasses, the shears and flat-iron,
The awl and knee-strap, the pint measure and quart measure, the
    counter and stool, the writing-pen of quill or metal, the making
    of all sorts of edged tools,
The brewery, brewing, the malt, the vats, everything that is done by
    brewers, wine-makers, vinegar-makers,
Leather-dressing, coach-making, boiler-making, rope-twisting, dis-
    tilling, sign-painting, lime-burning, cotton-picking, electro-
    plating, electrotyping, stereotyping,
Stave-machines, planing-machines, reaping-machines, ploughing-
    machines, thrashing-machines, steam wagons,
The cart of the carman, the omnibus, the ponderous dray,
Pyrotechny, letting off color'd fireworks at night, fancy figures and
    jets;
Beef on the butcher's stall, the slaughter-house of the butcher, the
    butcher in his killing-clothes,
The pens of live pork, the killing-hammer, the hog-hook, the
    scalder's tub, gutting, the cutter's cleaver, the packer's maul,
    and the plenteous winterwork of pork-packing,
Flour-works, grinding of wheat, rye, maize, rice, the barrels and the
    half and quarter barrels, the loaded barges, the high piles on
    wharves and levees,
The men and the work of the men on ferries, railroad, coasters, fish-
    boats, canals;
The hourly routine of your own or any man's life, the shop, yard,
    store, or factory,
These shows all near you by day and night—workman! whoever you
    are, your daily life!

In that and them the heft of the heaviest—in that and them far more
    than you estimated, (and far less also,)
In them realities for you and me, in them poems for you and me,
In them, not yourself—you and your soul enclose all things, regard-
    less of estimation,
In them the development good—in them all themes, hints, possi-
    bilities.

I do not affirm that what you see beyond is futile, I do not advise you
    to stop,
I do not say leadings you thought great are not great,
But I say that none lead to greater than these lead to.

6

Will you seek afar off? you surely come back at last,
In things best known to you finding the best, or as good as the best,
In folks nearest to you finding the sweetest, strongest, lovingest,
Happiness, knowledge, not in another place but this place, not for
    another hour but this hour,
Man in the first you see or touch, always in friend, brother, nighest
    neighbor—woman in mother, sister, wife,
The popular tastes and employments taking precedence in poems or
    anywhere,
You workwomen and workmen of these States having your own divine
    and strong life,
And all else giving place to men and women like you.

When the psalm sings instead of the singer,
When the script preaches instead of the preacher,
When the pulpit descends and goes instead of the carver that carved
    the supporting desk,
When I can touch the body of books by night or by day, and when
    they touch my body back again,
When a university course convinces like a slumbering woman and
    child convince,
When the minted gold in the vault smiles like the night-watchman's
    daughter,
When warrantee deeds loafe in chairs opposite and are my friendly
    companions,
I intend to reach them my hand, and make as much of them as I do of
    men and women like you.

1855   1881

A Song of the Rolling Earth

1

A song of the rolling earth, and of words according,
Were you thinking that those were the words, those upright lines?
    those curves, angles, dots?
No, those are not the words, the substantial words are in the ground
    and sea,
They are in the air, they are in you.

Were you thinking that those were the words, those delicious sounds
    out of your friends' mouths?
No, the real words are more delicious than they.

Human bodies are words, myriads of words,
(In the best poems re-appears the body, man's or woman's, well-
    shaped, natural, gay,
Every part able, active, receptive, without shame or the need of
    shame.)

Air, soil, water, fire—those are words,
I myself am a word with them—my qualities interpenetrate with
    theirs—my name is nothing to them,
Though it were told in the three thousand languages, what would air,
    soil, water, fire, know of my name?

A healthy presence, a friendly or commanding gesture, are words,
    sayings, meanings,
The charms that go with the mere looks of some men and women, are
    sayings and meanings also.

The workmanship of souls is by those inaudible words of the earth,
The masters know the earth's words and use them more than audible
    words.

Amelioration is one of the earth's words,
The earth neither lags nor hastens,
It has all attributes, growths, effects, latent in itself from the jump,
It is not half beautiful only, defects and excrescences show just as
    much as perfections show.

The earth does not withhold, it is generous enough,
The truths of the earth continually wait, they are not so conceal'd
    either,

They are calm, subtle, untransmissible by print,
They are imbued through all things conveying themselves will-
ingly,
Conveying a sentiment and invitation, I utter and utter,
I speak not, yet if you hear me not of what avail am I to you?
To bear, to better, lacking these of what avail am I?

(Accouche! accouchez!
Will you rot your own fruit in yourself there?
Will you squat and stifle there?)

The earth does not argue,
Is not pathetic, has no arrangements,
Does not scream, haste, persuade, threaten, promise,
Makes no discriminations, has no conceivable failures,
Closes nothing, refuses nothing, shuts none out,
Of all the powers, objects, states, it notifies, shuts none out.

The earth does not exhibit itself nor refuse to exhibit itself, pos-
sesses still underneath,
Underneath the ostensible sounds, the august chorus of heroes, the
wail of slaves,
Persuasions of lovers, curses, gasps of the dying, laughter of young
people, accents of bargainers,
Underneath these possessing words that never fail.

To her children the words of the eloquent dumb great mother never
fail,
The true words do not fail, for motion does not fail and reflection
does not fail,
Also the day and night do not fail, and the voyage we pursue does not
fail.

Of the interminable sisters,
Of the ceaseless cotillions of sisters,
Of the centripetal and centrifugal sisters, the elder and younger
sisters,
The beautiful sister we know dances on with the rest.

With her ample back towards every beholder,
With the fascinations of youth and the equal fascinations of age,
Sits she whom I too love like the rest, sits undisturb'd,
Holding up in her hand what has the character of a mirror, while her
eyes glance back from it,

Glance as she sits, inviting none, denying none,
Holding a mirror day and night tirelessly before her own face.

Seen at hand or seen at a distance,
Duly the twenty-four appear in public every day,
Duly approach and pass with their companions or a companion,
Looking from no countenances of their own, but from the counte-
    nances of those who are with them,
From the countenances of children or women or the manly counte-
    nance,
From the open countenances of animals or from inanimate things,
From the landscape or waters or from the exquisite apparition of
    the sky,
From our countenances, mine and yours, faithfully returning them,
Every day in public appearing without fail, but never twice with the
    same companions.

Embracing man, embracing all, proceed the three hundred and
    sixty-five resistlessly round the sun;
Embracing all, soothing, supporting, follow close three hundred and
    sixty-five offsets of the first, sure and necessary as they.

Tumbling on steadily, nothing dreading,
Sunshine, storm, cold, heat, forever withstanding, passing, car-
    rying,
The soul's realization and determination still inheriting,
The fluid vacuum around and ahead still entering and dividing,
No balk retarding, no anchor anchoring, on no rock striking,
Swift, glad, content, unbereav'd, nothing losing,
Of all able and ready at any time to give strict account,
The divine ship sails the divine sea.

2

Whoever you are! motion and reflection are especially for you,
The divine ship sails the divine sea for you.

Whoever you are! you are he or she for whom the earth is solid and
    liquid,
You are he or she for whom the sun and moon hang in the sky,
For none more than you are the present and the past,
For none more than you is immortality.

Each man to himself and each woman to herself, is the word of the
    past and present, and the true word of immortality;

No one can acquire for another—not one,
Not one can grow for another—not one.

The song is to the singer, and comes back most to him,
The teaching is to the teacher, and comes back most to him,
The murder is to the murderer, and comes back most to him,
The theft is to the thief, and comes back most to him,
The love is to the lover, and comes back most to him,
The gift is to the giver, and comes back most to him—it cannot fail,
The oration is to the orator, the acting is to the actor and actress not
    to the audience,
And no man understands any greatness or goodness but his own, or
    the indication of his own.

3

I swear the earth shall surely be complete to him or her who shall be
    complete,
The earth remains jagged and broken only to him or her who remains
    jagged and broken.

I swear there is no greatness or power that does not emulate those of
    the earth,
There can be no theory of any account unless it corroborate the
    theory of the earth,
No politics, song, religion, behavior, or what not, is of account,
    unless it compare with the amplitude of the earth,
Unless it face the exactness, vitality, impartiality, rectitude of the
    earth.

I swear I begin to see love with sweeter spasms than that which
    responds love,
It is that which contains itself, which never invites and never re-
    fuses.

I swear I begin to see little or nothing in audible words,
All merges toward the presentation of the unspoken meanings of the
    earth,
Toward him who sings the songs of the body and of the truths of the
    earth,
Toward him who makes the dictionaries of words that print cannot
    touch.

I swear I see what is better than to tell the best,
It is always to leave the best untold.

When I undertake to tell the best I find I cannot,
My tongue is ineffectual on its pivots,
My breath will not be obedient to its organs,
I become a dumb man.

The best of the earth cannot be told anyhow, all or any is best,
It is not what you anticipated, it is cheaper, easier, nearer,
Things are not dismiss'd from the places they held before,
The earth is just as positive and direct as it was before,
Facts, religions, improvements, politics, trades, are as real as be-
    fore,
But the soul is also real, it too is positive and direct,
No reasoning, no proof has establish'd it,
Undeniable growth has establish'd it.

4

These to echo the tones of souls and the phrases of souls,
(If they did not echo the phrases of souls what were they then?
If they had not reference to you in especial what were they then?)

I swear I will never henceforth have to do with the faith that tells the
    best,
I will have to do only with that faith that leaves the best untold.

Say on, sayers! sing on, singers!
Delve! mould! pile the words of the earth!
Work on, age after age, nothing is to be lost,
It may have to wait long, but it will certainly come in use,
When the materials are all prepared and ready, the architects shall
    appear.

I swear to you the architects shall appear without fail,
I swear to you they will understand you and justify you,
The greatest among them shall be he who best knows you, and
    encloses all and is faithful to all,
He and the rest shall not forget you, they shall perceive that you are
    not an iota less than they,
You shall be fully glorified in them.

1856   1881

Pioneers! O Pioneers!

Come my tan-faced children,
Follow well in order, get your weapons ready,
Have you your pistols? have you your sharp-edged axes?
Pioneers! O pioneers!

For we cannot tarry here,
We must march my darlings, we must bear the brunt of danger,
We the youthful sinewy races, all the rest on us depend,
Pioneers! O pioneers!

O you youths, Western youths,
So impatient, full of action, full of manly pride and friendship,
Plain I see you Western youths, see you tramping with the foremost,
Pioneers! O pioneers!

Have the elder races halted?
Do they droop and end their lesson, wearied over there beyond the
seas?
We take up the task eternal, and the burden and the lesson,
Pioneers! O pioneers!

All the past we leave behind,
We debouch upon a newer mightier world, varied world,
Fresh and strong the world we seize, world of labor and the march,
Pioneers! O pioneers!

We detachments steady throwing,
Down the edges, through the passes, up the mountains steep,
Conquering, holding, daring, venturing as we go the unknown ways,
Pioneers! O pioneers!

We primeval forests felling,
We the rivers stemming, vexing we and piercing deep the mines
within,
We the surface broad surveying, we the virgin soil upheaving,
Pioneers! O pioneers!

Colorado men are we,
From the peaks gigantic, from the great sierras and the high
plateaus,
From the mine and from the gully, from the hunting trail we come,
Pioneers! O pioneers!

From Nebraska, from Arkansas,
Central inland race are we, from Missouri, with the continental
    blood intervein'd,
All the hands of comrades clasping, all the Southern, all the
    Northern,
            Pioneers! O pioneers!

O resistless restless race!
O beloved race in all! O my breast aches with tender love for all!
O I mourn and yet exult, I am rapt with love for all,
            Pioneers! O pioneers!

Raise the mighty mother mistress,
Waving high the delicate mistress, over all the starry mistress, (bend
    your heads all,)
Raise the fang'd and warlike mistress, stern, impassive, weapon'd
    mistress,
            Pioneers! O pioneers!

See my children, resolute children,
By those swarms upon our rear we must never yield or falter,
Ages back in ghostly millions frowning there behind us urging,
            Pioneers! O pioneers!

On and on the compact ranks,
With accessions ever waiting, with the places of the dead quickly
    fill'd,
Through the battle, through defeat, moving yet and never stopping,
            Pioneers! O pioneers!

O to die advancing on!
Are there some of us to droop and die? has the hour come?
Then upon the march we fittest die, soon and sure the gap is fill'd,
            Pioneers! O pioneers!

All the pulses of the world,
Falling in they beat for us, with the Western movement beat,
Holding single or together, steady moving to the front, all for us,
            Pioneers! O pioneers!

Life's involv'd and varied pageants,
All the forms and shows, all the workmen at their work,
All the seamen and the landsmen, all the masters with their slaves,
            Pioneers! O pioneers!

All the hapless silent lovers,
All the prisoners in the prisons, all the righteous and the wicked,
All the joyous, all the sorrowing, all the living, all the dying,
    Pioneers! O pioneers!

I too with my soul and body,
We, a curious trio, picking, wandering on our way,
Through these shores amid the shadows, with the apparitions pressing,
    Pioneers! O pioneers!

Lo, the darting bowling orb!
Lo, the brother orbs around, all the clustering suns and planets,
All the dazzling days, all the mystic nights with dreams,
    Pioneers! O pioneers!

These are of us, they are with us,
All for primal needed work, while the followers there in embryo wait behind,
We to-day's procession heading, we the route for travel clearing,
    Pioneers! O pioneers!

O you daughters of the West!
O you young and elder daughters! O you mothers and you wives!
Never must you be divided, in our ranks you move united,
    Pioneers! O pioneers!

Minstrels latent on the prairies!
(Shrouded bards of other lands, you may rest, you have done your work,)
Soon I hear you coming warbling, soon you rise and tramp amid us,
    Pioneers! O pioneers!

Not for delectations sweet,
Not the cushion and the slipper, not the peaceful and the studious,
Not the riches safe and palling, not for us the tame enjoyment,
    Pioneers! O pioneers!

Do the feasters gluttonous feast?
Do the corpulent sleepers sleep? have they lock'd and bolted doors?
Still be ours the diet hard, and the blanket on the ground,
    Pioneers! O pioneers!

Has the night descended?
Was the road of late so toilsome? did we stop discouraged nodding on our way?

Yet a passing hour I yield you in your tracks to pause oblivious,
          Pioneers! O pioneers!

          Till with sound of trumpet,
Far, far off the daybreak call—hark! how loud and clear I hear
     it wind,
Swift! to the head of the army!—swift! spring to your places,
          Pioneers! O pioneers!

1865   1881

Out of the Cradle Endlessly Rocking

Out of the cradle endlessly rocking,
Out of the mocking-bird's throat, the musical shuttle,
Out of the Ninth-month midnight,
Over the sterile sands and the fields beyond, where the child leaving
     his bed wander'd alone, bareheaded, barefoot,
Down from the shower'd halo,
Up from the mystic play of shadows twining and twisting as if they
     were alive,
Out from the patches of briers and blackberries,
From the memories of the bird that chanted to me,
From your memories sad brother, from the fitful risings and fallings I
     heard,
From under that yellow half-moon late-risen and swollen as if with
     tears,
From those beginning notes of yearning and love there in the
     mist,
From the thousand responses of my heart never to cease,
From the myriad thence-arous'd words,
From the word stronger and more delicious than any,
From such as now they start the scene revisiting,
As a flock, twittering, rising, or overhead passing,
Borne hither, ere all eludes me, hurriedly,
A man, yet by these tears a little boy again,
Throwing myself on the sand, confronting the waves,
I, chanter of pains and joys, uniter of here and hereafter,
Taking all hints to use them, but swiftly leaping beyond them,
A reminiscence sing.

Once Paumanok,
When the lilac-scent was in the air and Fifth-month grass was
    growing,
Up this seashore in some briers,
Two feather'd guests from Alabama, two together,
And their nest, and four light-green eggs spotted with brown,
And every day the he-bird to and fro near at hand,
And every day the she-bird crouch'd on her nest, silent, with bright
    eyes,
And every day I, a curious boy, never too close, never disturbing
    them,
Cautiously peering, absorbing, translating.

Shine! shine! shine!
Pour down your warmth, great sun!
While we bask, we two together.

Two together!
Winds blow south, or winds blow north,
Day come white, or night come black,
Home, or rivers and mountains from home,
Singing all time, minding no time,
While we two keep together.

Till of a sudden,
May-be kill'd, unknown to her mate,
One forenoon the she-bird crouch'd not on the nest,
Nor return'd that afternoon, nor the next,
Nor ever appear'd again.

And thenceforward all summer in the sound of the sea,
And at night under the full of the moon in calmer weather,
Over the hoarse surging of the sea,
Or flitting from brier to brier by day,
I saw, I heard at intervals the remaining one, the he-bird,
The solitary guest from Alabama.

Blow! blow! blow!
Blow up sea-winds along Paumanok's shore;
I wait and I wait till you blow my mate to me.

Yes, when the stars glisten'd,
All night long on the prong of a moss-scallop'd stake,
Down almost amid the slapping waves,
Sat the lone singer wonderful causing tears.

He call'd on his mate,
He pour'd forth the meanings which I of all men know.

Yes my brother I know,
The rest might not, but I have treasur'd every note,
For more than once dimly down to the beach gliding,
Silent, avoiding the moonbeams, blending myself with the shadows,
Recalling now the obscure shapes, the echoes, the sounds and sights
    after their sorts,
The white arms out in the breakers tirelessly tossing,
I, with bare feet, a child, the wind wafting my hair,
Listen'd long and long.

Listen'd to keep, to sing, now translating the notes,
Following you my brother.

Soothe! soothe! soothe!
Close on its wave soothes the wave behind,
And again another behind embracing and lapping, every one
    close,
But my love soothes not me, not me.

Low hangs the moon, it rose late,
It is lagging—O I think it is heavy with love, with love.

O madly the sea pushes upon the land,
With love, with love.

O night! do I not see my love fluttering out among the breakers?
What is that little black thing I see there in the white?

Loud! loud! loud!
Loud I call to you, my love!
High and clear I shoot my voice over the waves,
Surely you must know who is here, is here,
You must know who I am, my love.

Low-hanging moon!
What is that dusky spot in your brown yellow?
O it is the shape, the shape of my mate!
O moon do not keep her from me any longer.

Land! land! O land!
Whichever way I turn, O I think you could give me my mate back
    again if you only would,
For I am almost sure I see her dimly whichever way I look.

O rising stars!
Perhaps the one I want so much will rise, will rise with some of you.

O throat! O trembling throat!
Sound clearer through the atmosphere!
Pierce the woods, the earth,
Somewhere listening to catch you must be the one I want.

Shake out carols!
Solitary here, the night's carols!
Carols of lonesome love! death's carols!
Carols under that lagging, yellow, waning moon!
O under that moon where she droops almost down into the sea!
O reckless despairing carols.

But soft! sink low!
Soft! let me just murmur,
And do you wait a moment you husky-nois'd sea,
For somewhere I believe I heard my mate responding to me,
So faint, I must be still, be still to listen,
But not altogether still, for then she might not come immediately to me.

Hither my love!
Here I am! here!
With this just-sustain'd note I announce myself to you,
This gentle call is for you my love, for you.

Do not be decoy'd elsewhere,
That is the whistle of the wind, it is not my voice,
That is the fluttering, the fluttering of the spray,
Those are the shadows of leaves.

O darkness! O in vain!
O I am very sick and sorrowful.

O brown halo in the sky near the moon, drooping upon the sea!
O troubled reflection in the sea!
O throat! O throbbing heart!
And I singing uselessly, uselessly all the night.

O past! O happy life! O songs of joy!
In the air, in the woods, over fields,
Loved! loved! loved! loved! loved!
But my mate no more, no more with me!
We two together no more.

The aria sinking,
All else continuing, the stars shining,
The winds blowing, the notes of the bird continuous echoing,
With angry moans the fierce old mother incessantly moaning,
On the sands of Paumanok's shore gray and rustling,
The yellow half-moon enlarged, sagging down, drooping, the face of
    the sea almost touching,
The boy ecstatic, with his bare feet the waves, with his hair the
    atmosphere dallying,
The love in the heart long pent, now loose, now at last tumultuously
    bursting,
The aria's meaning, the ears, the soul, swiftly depositing,
The strange tears down the cheeks coursing,
The colloquy there, the trio, each uttering,
The undertone, the savage old mother incessantly crying,
To the boy's soul's questions sullenly timing, some drown'd secret
    hissing,
To the outsetting bard.

Demon or bird! (said the boy's soul,)
Is it indeed toward your mate you sing? or is it really to me?
For I, that was a child, my tongue's use sleeping, now I have
    heard you,
Now in a moment I know what I am for, I awake,
And already a thousand singers, a thousand songs, clearer, louder
    and more sorrowful than yours,
A thousand warbling echoes have started to life within me, never
    to die.

O you singer solitary, singing by yourself, projecting me,
O solitary me listening, never more shall I cease perpetuating you,
Never more shall I escape, never more the reverberations,
Never more the cries of unsatisfied love be absent from me,
Never again leave me to be the peaceful child I was before what there
    in the night,
By the sea under the yellow and sagging moon,
The messenger there arous'd, the fire, the sweet hell within,
The unknown want, the destiny of me.

O give me the clew! (it lurks in the night here somewhere,)
O if I am to have so much, let me have more!

A word then, (for I will conquer it,)
The word final, superior to all,

Subtle, sent up—what is it?—I listen;
Are you whispering it, and have been all the time, you sea waves?
Is that it from your liquid rims and wet sands?

Whereto answering, the sea,
Delaying not, hurrying not,
Whisper'd me through the night, and very plainly before daybreak,
Lisp'd to me the low and delicious word death,
And again death, death, death, death,
Hissing melodious, neither like the bird nor like my arous'd child's
    heart,
But edging near as privately for me rustling at my feet,
Creeping thence steadily up to my ears and laving me softly all over,
Death, death, death, death, death.

Which I do not forget,
But fuse the song of my dusky demon and brother,
That he sang to me in the moonlight on Paumanok's gray beach,
With the thousand responsive songs at random,
My own songs awaked from that hour,
And with them the key, the word up from the waves,
The word of the sweetest song and all songs,
That strong and delicious word which, creeping to my feet,
(Or like some old crone rocking the cradle, swathed in sweet gar-
    ments, bending aside,)
The sea whisper'd me.

1859   1881

Beat! Beat! Drums!

Beat! beat! drums!—blow! bugles! blow!
Through the windows—through doors—burst like a ruthless force,
Into the solemn church, and scatter the congregation,
Into the school where the scholar is studying;
Leave not the bridegroom quiet—no happiness must he have now
    with his bride,
Nor the peaceful farmer any peace, ploughing his field or gathering
    his grain,
So fierce you whirr and pound you drums—so shrill you bugles blow.

Beat! beat! drums!—blow! bugles! blow!
Over the traffic of cities—over the rumble of wheels in the streets;
Are beds prepared for sleepers at night in the houses? no sleepers
    must sleep in those beds,
No bargainers' bargains by day—no brokers or speculators—would
    they continue?
Would the talkers be talking? would the singer attempt to sing?
Would the lawyer rise in the court to state his case before the judge?
Then rattle quicker, heavier drums—you bugles wilder blow.

Beat! beat! drums!—blow! bugles! blow!
Make no parley—stop for no expostulation,
Mind not the timid—mind not the weeper or prayer,
Mind not the old man beseeching the young man,
Let not the child's voice be heard, nor the mother's entreaties,
Make even the trestles to shake the dead where they lie awaiting the
    hearses,
So strong you thump O terrible drums—so loud you bugles blow.
1861   1867

The Wound-Dresser

1

An old man bending I come among new faces,
Years looking backward resuming in answer to children,
Come tell us old man, as from young men and maidens that love me,
(Arous'd and angry, I'd thought to beat the alarum, and urge relent-
    less war,
But soon my fingers fail'd me, my face droop'd and I resign'd myself,
To sit by the wounded and soothe them, or silently watch the dead;)
Years hence of these scenes, of these furious passions, these
    chances,
Of unsurpass'd heroes, (was one side so brave? the other was equally
    brave;)
Now be witness again, paint the mightiest armies of earth,
Of those armies so rapid so wondrous what saw you to tell us?
What stays with you latest and deepest? of curious panics,
Of hard-fought engagements or sieges tremendous what deepest
    remains?

2

O maidens and young men I love and that love me,
What you ask of my days those the strangest and sudden your talking
   recalls,
Soldier alert I arrive after a long march cover'd with sweat and dust,
In the nick of time I come, plunge in the fight, loudly shout in the
   rush of successful charge,
Enter the captur'd works—yet lo, like a swift running river they fade,
Pass and are gone they fade—I dwell not on soldiers' perils or
   soldiers' joys,
(Both I remember well—many of the hardships, few the joys, yet I
   was content.)

But in silence, in dreams' projections,
While the world of gain and appearance and mirth goes on,
So soon what is over forgotten, and waves wash the imprints off the
   sand,
With hinged knees returning I enter the doors, (while for you up there,
Whoever you are, follow without noise and be of strong heart.)

Bearing the bandages, water and sponge,
Straight and swift to my wounded I go,
Where they lie on the ground after the battle brought in,
Where their priceless blood reddens the grass the ground,
Or to the rows of the hospital tent, or under the roof'd hospital,
To the long rows of cots up and down each side I return,
To each and all one after another I draw near, not one do I miss,
An attendant follows holding a tray, he carries a refuse pail,
Soon to be fill'd with clotted rags and blood, emptied, and fill'd
   again.

I onward go, I stop,
With hinged knees and steady hand to dress wounds,
I am firm with each, the pangs are sharp yet unavoidable,
One turns to me his appealing eyes—poor boy! I never knew you,
Yet I think I could not refuse this moment to die for you, if that would
   save you.

3

On, on I go, (open doors of time! open hospital doors!)
The crush'd head I dress, (poor crazed hand tear not the bandage
   away,)

The neck of the cavalry-man with the bullet through and through I
    examine,
Hard the breathing rattles, quite glazed already the eye, yet life
    struggles hard,
(Come sweet death! be persuaded O beautiful death!
In mercy come quickly.)

From the stump of the arm, the amputated hand,
I undo the clotted lint, remove the slough, wash off the matter and
    blood,
Back on his pillow the soldier bends with curv'd neck and side
    falling head,
His eyes are closed, his face is pale, he dares not look on the bloody
    stump,
And has not yet look'd on it.

I dress a wound in the side, deep, deep,
But a day or two more, for see the frame all wasted and sink-
    ing,
And the yellow-blue countenance see.

I dress the perforated shoulder, the foot with the bullet-wound,
Cleanse the one with a gnawing and putrid gangrene, so sickening,
    so offensive,
While the attendant stands behind aside me holding the tray and
    pail.

I am faithful, I do not give out,
The fractur'd thigh, the knee, the wound in the abdomen,
These and more I dress with impassive hand, (yet deep in my breast
    a fire, a burning flame.)

4

Thus in silence in dreams' projections,
Returning, resuming, I thread my way through the hospitals,
The hurt and wounded I pacify with soothing hand,
I sit by the restless all the dark night, some are so young,
Some suffer so much, I recall the experience sweet and sad,
(Many a soldier's loving arms about this neck have cross'd and
    rested,
Many a soldier's kiss dwells on these bearded lips.)

1865   1881

When Lilacs Last in the Dooryard Bloom'd

1

When lilacs last in the dooryard bloom'd,
And the great star early droop'd in the western sky in the night,
I mourn'd, and yet shall mourn with ever-returning spring.

Ever-returning spring, trinity sure to me you bring,
Lilac blooming perennial and drooping star in the west,
And thought of him I love.

2

O powerful western fallen star!
O shades of night—O moody, tearful night!
O great star disappear'd—O the black murk that hides the star!
O cruel hands that hold me powerless—O helpless soul of me!
O harsh surrounding cloud that will not free my soul.

3

In the dooryard fronting an old farm-house near the whitewash'd
    palings,
Stands the lilac-bush tall-growing with heart-shaped leaves of rich
    green,
With many a pointed blossom rising delicate, with the perfume
    strong I love,
With every leaf a miracle—and from this bush in the dooryard,
With delicate-color'd blossoms and heart-shaped leaves of rich green,
A sprig with its flower I break.

4

In the swamp in secluded recesses,
A shy and hidden bird is warbling a song.

Solitary the thrush,
The hermit withdrawn to himself, avoiding the settlements,
Sings by himself a song.

Song of the bleeding throat,
Death's outlet song of life, (for well dear brother I know,
If thou wast not granted to sing thou would'st surely die.)

5

Over the breast of the spring, the land, amid cities,
Amid lanes and through old woods, where lately the violets peep'd
     from the ground, spotting the gray debris,
Amid the grass in the fields each side of the lanes, passing the
     endless grass,
Passing the yellow-spear'd wheat, every grain from its shroud in the
     dark-brown fields uprisen,
Passing the apple-tree blows of white and pink in the orchards,
Carrying a corpse to where it shall rest in the grave,
Night and day journeys a coffin.

6

Coffin that passes through lanes and streets,
Through day and night with the great cloud darkening the land,
With the pomp of the inloop'd flags with the cities draped in black,
With the show of the States themselves as of crape-veil'd women
     standing,
With processions long and winding and the flambeaus of the night,
With the countless torches lit, with the silent sea of faces and the
     unbared heads,
With the waiting depot, the arriving coffin, and the sombre faces,
With dirges through the night, with the thousand voices rising strong
     and solemn,
With all the mournful voices of the dirges pour'd around the coffin,
The dim-lit churches and the shuddering organs—where amid these
     you journey,
With the tolling tolling bells' perpetual clang,
Here, coffin that slowly passes,
I give you my sprig of lilac.

7

(Nor for you, for one alone,
Blossoms and branches green to coffins all I bring,
For fresh as the morning, thus would I chant a song for you O sane
     and sacred death.

All over bouquets of roses,
O death, I cover you over with roses and early lilies,
But mostly and now the lilac that blooms the first,
Copious I break, I break the sprigs from the bushes,

With loaded arms I come, pouring for you,
For you and the coffins all of you O death.)

8

O western orb sailing the heaven,
Now I know what you must have meant as a month since I walk'd,
As I walk'd in silence the transparent shadowy night,
As I saw you had something to tell as you bent to me night after
    night,
As you droop'd from the sky low down as if to my side, (while the
    other stars all look'd on,)
As we wander'd together the solemn night, (for something I know not
    what kept me from sleep,)
As the night advanced, and I saw on the rim of the west how full you
    were of woe,
As I stood on the rising ground in the breeze in the cool transparent
    night,
As I watch'd where you pass'd and was lost in the netherward black
    of the night,
As my soul in its trouble dissatisfied sank, as where you sad
    orb,
Concluded, dropt in the night, and was gone.

9

Sing on there in the swamp,
O singer bashful and tender, I hear your notes, I hear your call,
I hear, I come presently, I understand you,
But a moment I linger, for the lustrous star has detain'd me,
The star my departing comrade holds and detains me.

10

O how shall I warble myself for the dead one there I loved?
And how shall I deck my song for the large sweet soul that has
    gone?
And what shall my perfume be for the grave of him I love?

Sea-winds blown from east and west,
Blown from the Eastern sea and blown from the Western sea, till
    there on the prairies meeting,
These and with these and the breath of my chant,
I'll perfume the grave of him I love.

11

O what shall I hang on the chamber walls?
And what shall the pictures be that I hang on the walls,
To adorn the burial-house of him I love?

Pictures of growing spring and farms and homes,
With the Fourth-month eve at sundown, and the gray smoke lucid
  and bright,
With floods of the yellow gold of the gorgeous, indolent, sinking sun,
  burning, expanding the air,
With the fresh sweet herbage under foot, and the pale green leaves of
  the trees prolific,
In the distance the flowing glaze, the breast of the river, with a wind-
  dapple here and there,
With ranging hills on the banks, with many a line against the sky,
  and shadows,
And the city at hand with dwellings so dense, and stacks of chim-
  neys,
And all the scenes of life and the workshops, and the workmen
  homeward returning.

12

Lo, body and soul—this land,
My own Manhattan with spires, and the sparkling and hurrying
  tides, and the ships,
The varied and ample land, the South and the North in the light,
  Ohio's shores and flashing Missouri,
And ever the far-spreading prairies cover'd with grass and corn.

Lo, the most excellent sun so calm and haughty,
The violet and purple morn with just-felt breezes,
The gentle soft-born measureless light,
The miracle spreading bathing all, the fulfill'd noon,
The coming eve delicious, the welcome night and the stars,
Over my cities shining all, enveloping man and land.

13

Sing on, sing on you gray-brown bird,
Sing from the swamps, the recesses, pour your chant from the
  bushes,
Limitless out of the dusk, out of the cedars and pines.

Sing on dearest brother, warble your reedy song,
Loud human song, with voice of uttermost woe.

O liquid and free and tender!
O wild and loose to my soul—O wondrous singer!
You only I hear—yet the star holds me, (but will soon depart,)
Yet the lilac with mastering odor holds me.

14

Now while I sat in the day and look'd forth,
In the close of the day with its light and the fields of spring, and the
    farmers preparing their crops,
In the large unconscious scenery of my land with its lakes and
    forests,
In the heavenly aerial beauty, (after the perturb'd winds and the
    storms,)
Under the arching heavens of the afternoon swift passing, and the
    voices of children and women,
The many-moving sea-tides, and I saw the ships how they sail'd,
And the summer approaching with richness, and the fields all busy
    with labor,
And the infinite separate houses, how they all went on, each with its
    meals and minutia of daily usages,
And the streets how their throbbings throbb'd, and the cities pent—
    lo, then and there,
Falling upon them all and among them all, enveloping me with the
    rest,
Appear'd the cloud, appear'd the long black trail,
And I knew death, its thought, and the sacred knowledge of death.

Then with the knowledge of death as walking one side of me,
And the thought of death close-walking the other side of me,
And I in the middle as with companions, and as holding the hands of
    companions,
I fled forth to the hiding receiving night that talks not,
Down to the shores of the water, the path by the swamp in the
    dimness,
To the solemn shadowy cedars and ghostly pines so still.

And the singer so shy to the rest receiv'd me,
The gray-brown bird I know receiv'd us comrades three,
And he sang the carol of death, and a verse for him I love.

From deep secluded recesses,
From the fragrant cedars and the ghostly pines so still,
Came the carol of the bird.

And the charm of the carol rapt me,
As I held as if by their hands my comrades in the night,
And the voice of my spirit tallied the song of the bird.

Come lovely and soothing death,
Undulate round the world, serenely arriving, arriving,
In the day, in the night, to all, to each,
Sooner or later delicate death.

Prais'd be the fathomless universe,
For life and joy, and for objects and knowledge curious,
And for love, sweet love—but praise! praise! praise!
For the sure-enwinding arms of cool-enfolding death.

Dark mother always gliding near with soft feet,
Have none chanted for thee a chant of fullest welcome?
Then I chant it for thee, I glorify thee above all,
I bring thee a song that when thou must indeed come, come un-
    falteringly.

Approach strong deliveress,
When it is so, when thou hast taken them I joyously sing the dead,
Lost in the loving floating ocean of thee,
Laved in the flood of thy bliss O death.

From me to thee glad serenades,
Dances for thee I propose saluting thee, adornments and feastings for
    thee,
And the sights of the open landscape and the high-spread sky are
    fitting,
And life and the fields, and the huge and thoughtful night.

The night in silence under many a star,
The ocean shore and the husky whispering wave whose voice I know,
And the soul turning to thee O vast and well-veil'd death,
And the body gratefully nestling close to thee.

Over the tree-tops I float thee a song,
Over the rising and sinking waves, over the myriad fields and the
    prairies wide,
Over the dense-pack'd cities all and the teeming wharves and ways,
I float this carol with joy, with joy to thee O death.

15

To the tally of my soul,
Loud and strong kept up the gray-brown bird,
With pure deliberate notes spreading filling the night.

Loud in the pines and cedars dim,
Clear in the freshness moist and the swamp-perfume,
And I with my comrades there in the night.

While my sight that was bound in my eyes unclosed,
As to long panoramas of visions.

And I saw askant the armies,
I saw as in noiseless dreams hundreds of battle-flags,
Borne through the smoke of the battles and pierc'd with missiles I
    saw them,
And carried hither and yon through the smoke, and torn and bloody,
And at last but a few shreds left on the staffs, (and all in silence,)
And the staffs all splinter'd and broken.

I saw battle-corpses, myriads of them,
And the white skeletons of young men, I saw them,
I saw the debris and debris of all the slain soldiers of the war,
But I saw they were not as was thought,
They themselves were fully at rest, they suffer'd not,
The living remain'd and suffer'd, the mother suffer'd,
And the wife and the child and the musing comrade suffer'd,
And the armies that remain'd suffer'd.

16

Passing the visions, passing the night,
Passing, unloosing the hold of my comrades' hands,
Passing the song of the hermit bird and the tallying song of my soul,
Victorious song, death's outlet song, yet varying ever-altering song,
As low and wailing, yet clear the notes, rising and falling, flooding
    the night,
Sadly sinking and fainting, as warning and warning, and yet again
    bursting with joy,
Covering the earth and filling the spread of the heaven,
As that powerful psalm in the night I heard from recesses,
Passing, I leave thee lilac with heart-shaped leaves,
I leave thee there in the dooryard, blooming, returning with spring.

I cease from my song for thee,
From my gaze on thee in the west, fronting the west, communing
    with thee,
O comrade lustrous with silver face in the night.

Yet each to keep and all, retrievements out of the night,
The song, the wondrous chant of the gray-brown bird,
And the tallying chant, the echo arous'd in my soul,
With the lustrous and drooping star with the countenance full of woe,
With the holders holding my hand nearing the call of the bird,
Comrades mine and I in the midst, and their memory ever to keep,
    for the dead I loved so well,
For the sweetest, wisest soul of all my days and lands—and this for
    his dear sake,
Lilac and star and bird twined with the chant of my soul,
There in the fragrant pines and the cedars dusk and dim.

1865–6   1881

O Captain! My Captain!

O Captain! my Captain! our fearful trip is done,
The ship has weather'd every rack, the prize we sought is won,
The port is near, the bells I hear, the people all exulting,
While follow eyes the steady keel, the vessel grim and daring;
       But O heart! heart! heart!
         O the bleeding drops of red,
           Where on the deck my Captain lies,
            Fallen cold and dead.

O Captain! my Captain! rise up and hear the bells;
Rise up—for you the flag is flung—for you the bugle trills,
For you bouquets and ribbon'd wreaths—for you the shores a-crowding,
For you they call, the swaying mass, their eager faces turning;
       Here Captain! dear father!
        The arm beneath your head!
         It is some dream that on the deck,
          You've fallen cold and dead.

My Captain does not answer, his lips are pale and still,
My father does not feel my arm, he has no pulse nor will,
The ship is anchor'd safe and sound, its voyage closed and done,

From fearful trip the victor ship comes in with object won:
> Exult O shores, and ring O bells!
>> But I with mournful tread,
>>> Walk the deck my Captain lies,
>>>> Fallen cold and dead.

1865   1871

By Blue Ontario's Shore

1

By blue Ontario's shore,
As I mused of these warlike days and of peace return'd, and the dead
    that return no more,
A Phantom gigantic superb, with stern visage accosted me,
Chant me the poem, it said, *that comes from the soul of America,
    chant me the carol of victory,*
And strike up the marches of Libertad, marches more powerful yet,
And sing me before you go the song of the throes of Democracy.

(Democracy, the destin'd conqueror, yet treacherous lip-smiles
    everywhere,
And death and infidelity at every step.)

2

A Nation announcing itself,
I myself make the only growth by which I can be appreciated,
I reject none, accept all, then reproduce all in my own forms.

A breed whose proof is in time and deeds,
What we are we are, nativity is answer enough to objections,
We wield ourselves as a weapon is wielded,
We are powerful and tremendous in ourselves,
We are executive in ourselves, we are sufficient in the variety of
    ourselves,
We are the most beautiful to ourselves and in ourselves,
We stand self-pois'd in the middle, branching thence over the
    world,
From Missouri, Nebraska, or Kansas, laughing attacks to scorn.

Nothing is sinful to us outside of ourselves,

Whatever appears, whatever does not appear, we are beautiful or
    sinful in ourselves only.

(O Mother—O Sisters dear!
If we are lost, no victor else has destroy'd us,
It is by ourselves we go down to eternal night.)

3

Have you thought there could be but a single supreme?
There can be any number of supremes—one does not countervail
    another any more than one eyesight countervails another, or
    one life countervails another.

All is eligible to all,
All is for individuals, all is for you,
No condition is prohibited, not God's or any.

All comes by the body, only health puts you rapport with the
    universe.

Produce great Persons, the rest follows.

4

Piety and conformity to them that like,
Peace, obesity, allegiance, to them that like,
I am he who tauntingly compels men, women, nations,
Crying, Leap from your seats and contend for your lives!

I am he who walks the States with a barb'd tongue, questioning every
    one I meet,
Who are you that wanted only to be told what you knew before?
Who are you that wanted only a book to join you in your nonsense?

(With pangs and cries as thine own O bearer of many children,
These clamors wild to a race of pride I give.)
O lands, would you be freer than all that has ever been before?
If you would be freer than all that has been before, come listen
    to me.

Fear grace, elegance, civilization, delicatesse,
Fear the mellow sweet, the sucking of honey-juice,
Beware the advancing mortal ripening of Nature,
Beware what precedes the decay of the ruggedness of states
    and men.

5

Ages, precedents, have long been accumulating undirected mate-
rials,
America brings builders, and brings its own styles.

The immortal poets of Asia and Europe have done their work and
pass'd to other spheres,
A work remains, the work of surpassing all they have done.

America, curious toward foreign characters, stands by its own at all
hazards,
Stands removed, spacious, composite, sound, initiates the true use
of precedents,
Does not repel them or the past or what they have produced under
their forms,
Takes the lesson with calmness, perceives the corpse slowly borne
from the house,
Perceives that it waits a little while in the door, that it was fittest for
its days,
That its life has descended to the stalwart and well-shaped heir who
approaches,
And that he shall be fittest for his days.

Any period one nation must lead,
One land must be the promise and reliance of the future.

These States are the amplest poem,
Here is not merely a nation but a teeming Nation of nations,
Here the doings of men correspond with the broadcast doings of the
day and night,
Here is what moves in magnificent masses careless of particulars,
Here are the roughs, beards, friendliness, combativeness, the soul
loves,
Here the flowing trains, here the crowds, equality, diversity, the soul
loves.

6

Land of lands and bards to corroborate!
Of them standing among them, one lifts to the light a west-bred face,
To him the hereditary countenance bequeath'd both mother's and
father's,
His first parts substances, earth, water, animals, trees,
Built of the common stock, having room for far and near,

Used to dispense with other lands, incarnating this land,
Attracting it body and soul to himself, hanging on its neck with
    incomparable love,
Plunging his seminal muscle into its merits and demerits,
Making its cities, beginnings, events, diversities, wars, vocal
    in him,
Making its rivers, lakes, bays, embouchure in him,
Mississippi with yearly freshets and changing chutes, Columbia,
    Niagara, Hudson, spending themselves lovingly in him,
If the Atlantic coast stretch or the Pacific coast stretch, he stretching
    with them North or South,
Spanning between them East and West, and touching whatever is
    between them,
Growths growing from him to offset the growths of pine, cedar,
    hemlock, live-oak, locust, chestnut, hickory, cottonwood, or-
    ange, magnolia,
Tangles as tangled in him as any cranebake or swamp,
He likening sides and peaks of mountains, forests coated with
    northern transparent ice,
Off him pasturage sweet and natural as savanna, upland, prairie,
Through him flights, whirls, screams, answering those of the fish-
    hawk, mocking-bird, night-heron, and eagle,
His spirit surrounding his country's spirit, unclosed to good and
    evil,
Surrounding the essences of real things, old times and present
    times,
Surrounding just found shores, islands, tribes of red aborigines,
Weather-beaten vessels, landings, settlements, embryo stature and
    muscle,
The haughty defiance of the Year One, war, peace, the formation of
    the Constitution,
The separate States, the simple elastic scheme, the immigrants,
The Union always swarming with blatherers and always sure and
    impregnable,
The unsurvey'd interior, log-houses, clearings, wild animals,
    hunters, trappers,
Surrounding the multiform agriculture, mines, temperature, the
    gestation of new States,
Congress convening every Twelfth-month, the members duly coming
    up from the uttermost parts,
Surrounding the noble character of mechanics and farmers, espe-
    cially the young men,

Responding their manners, speech, dress, friendships, the gait they
have of persons who never knew how it felt to stand in the
presence of superiors,
The freshness and candor of their physiognomy, the copiousness and
decision of their phrenology,
The picturesque looseness of their carriage, their fierceness when
wrong'd,
The fluency of their speech, their delight in music, their curiosity,
good temper and open-handedness, the whole composite make,
The prevailing ardor and enterprise, the large amativeness,
The perfect equality of the female with the male, the fluid movement
of the population,
The superior marine, free commerce, fisheries, whaling, gold-
digging,
Wharf-hemm'd cities, railroad and steamboat lines intersecting all
points,
Factories, mercantile life, labor-saving machinery, the Northeast,
Northwest, Southwest,
Manhattan firemen, the Yankee swap, southern plantation life,
Slavery—the murderous, treacherous conspiracy to raise it upon
the ruins of all the rest,
On and on to the grapple with it—Assassin! then your life or ours be
the stake, and respite no more.

7

(Lo, high toward heaven, this day,
Libertad, from the conqueress' field return'd,
I mark the new aureola around your head,
No more of soft astral, but dazzling and fierce,
With war's flames and the lambent lightnings playing,
And your port immovable where you stand,
With still the inextinguishable glance and the clinch'd and lifted
fist,
And your foot on the neck of the menacing one, the scorner utterly
crush'd beneath you,
The menacing arrogant one that strode and advanced with his sense-
less scorn, bearing the murderous knife,
The wide-swelling one, the braggart that would yesterday do so
much,
To-day a carrion dead and damn'd, the despised of all the earth,
An offal rank, to the dunghill maggots spurn'd.)

Others take finish, but the Republic is ever constructive and ever
    keeps vista,
Others adorn the past, but you O days of the present, I adorn you,
O days of the future I believe in you—I isolate myself for your sake,
O America because you build for mankind I build for you,
O well-beloved stone-cutters, I lead them who plan with decision
    and science,
Lead the present with friendly hand toward the future.

(Bravas to all impulses sending sane children to the next age!
But damn that which spends itself with no thought of the stain,
    pains, dismay, feebleness, it is bequeathing.)

9

I listened to the Phantom by Ontario's shore,
I heard the voice arising demanding bards,
By them all native and grand, by them alone can these States be
    fused into the compact organism of a Nation.

To hold men together by paper and seal or by compulsion is no
    account,
That only holds men together which aggregates all in a living princi-
    ple, as the hold of the limbs of the body or the fibres of plants.

Of all races and eras these States with veins full of poetical stuff most
    need poets, and are to have the greatest, and use them the
    greatest,
Their Presidents shall not be their common referee so much as their
    poets shall.

(Soul of love and tongue of fire!
Eye to pierce the deepest deeps and sweep the world!
Ah Mother, prolific and full in all besides, yet how long barren,
    barren?)

10

Of these States the poet is the equable man,
Not in him but off from him things are grotesque, eccentric, fail of
    their full returns,
Nothing out of its place is good, nothing in its place is bad,
He bestows on every object or quality its fit proportion, neither more
    nor less,

He is the arbiter of the diverse, he is the key,
He is the equalizer of his age and land,
He supplies what wants supplying, he checks what wants checking,
In peace out of him speaks the spirit of peace, large, rich, thrifty,
      building populous towns, encouraging agriculture, arts, com-
      merce, lighting the study of man, the soul, health, immortality,
      government,
In war he is the best backer of the war, he fetches artillery as good as
      the engineer's, he can make every word he speaks draw blood,
The years straying toward infidelity he withholds by his steady faith,
He is no arguer, he is judgment, (Nature accepts him absolutely,)
He judges not as the judge judges but as the sun falling round a
      helpless thing,
As he sees the farthest he has the most faith,
His thoughts are the hymns of the praise of things,
In the dispute on God and eternity he is silent,
He sees eternity less like a play with a prologue and denouement,
He sees eternity in men and women, he does not see men and women
      as dreams or dots.

For the great Idea, the idea of perfect and free individuals,
For that, the bard walks in advance, leader of leaders,
The attitude of him cheers up slaves and horrifies foreign despots.

Without extinction is Liberty, without retrograde is Equality,
They live in the feelings of young men and the best women,
(Not for nothing have the indomitable heads of the earth been always
      ready to fall for Liberty.)

11

For the great Idea,
That, O my brethren, that is the mission of poets.

Songs of stern defiance ever ready,
Songs of the rapid arming and the march,
The flag of peace quick-folded, and instead the flag we know,
Warlike flag of the great Idea.

(Angry cloth I saw there leaping!
I stand again in leaden rain your flapping folds saluting,
I sing you over all, flying beckoning through the fight—O the hard-
      contested fight!
The cannons ope their rosy-flashing muzzles—the hurtled balls
      scream,

The battle-front forms amid the smoke—the volleys pour incessant from the line,
Hark, the ringing word *Charge!*—now the tussle and the furious maddening yells,
Now the corpses tumble curl'd upon the ground,
Cold, cold in death, for precious life of you,
Angry cloth I saw there leaping.)

12

Are you he who would assume a place to teach or be a poet here in the States?
The place is august, the terms obdurate.

Who would assume to teach here may well prepare himself body and mind,
He may well survey, ponder, arm, fortify, harden, make lithe himself,
He shall surely be question'd beforehand by me with many and stern questions.

Who are you indeed who would talk or sing to America?
Have you studied out the land, its idioms and men?
Have you learn'd the physiology, phrenology, politics, geography, pride, freedom, friendship of the land? its substratums and objects?
Have you consider'd the organic compact of the first day of the first year of Independence, sign'd by the Commissioners, ratified by the States, and read by Washington at the head of the army?
Have you possess'd yourself of the Federal Constitution?
Do you see who have left all feudal processes and poems behind them, and assumed the poems and processes of Democracy?
Are you faithful to things? do you teach what the land and sea, the bodies of men, womanhood, amativeness, heroic angers, teach?
Have you sped through fleeting customs, popularities?
Can you hold your hand against all seductions, follies, whirls, fierce contentions? are you very strong? are you really of the whole People?
Are you not of some coterie? some school or mere religion?
Are you done with reviews and criticisms of life? animating now to life itself?

Have you vivified yourself from the maternity of these States?
Have you too the old ever-fresh forbearance and impartiality?
Do you hold the like love for those hardening to maturity? for the
    last-born? little and big? and for the errant?

What is this you bring my America?
Is it uniform with my country?
Is it not something that has been better told or done before?
Have you not imported this or the spirit of it in some ship?
Is it not a mere tale? a rhyme? a prettiness?—is the good old cause
    in it?
Has it not dangled long at the heels of the poets, politicians, literats,
    of enemies' lands?
Does it not assume that what is notoriously gone is still here?
Does it answer universal needs? will it improve manners?
Does it sound with trumpet-voice the proud victory of the Union in
    that secession war?
Can your performance face the open fields and the seaside?
Will it absorb into me as I absorb food, air, to appear again in my
    strength, gait, face?
Have real employments contributed to it? original makers, not mere
    amanuenses?
Does it meet modern discoveries, calibres, facts, face to face?
What does it mean to American persons, progresses, cities? Chi-
    cago, Kanada, Arkansas?
Does it see behind the apparent custodians the real custodians
    standing, menacing, silent, the mechanics, Manhattanese,
    Western men, Southerners, significant alike in their apathy,
    and in the promptness of their love?
Does it see what finally befalls, and has always finally befallen, each
    temporizer, patcher, outsider, partialist, alarmist, infidel, who
    has ever ask'd any thing of America?
What mocking and scornful negligence?
The track strew'd with the dust of skeletons,
By the roadside others disdainfully toss'd.

13

Rhymes and rhymers pass away, poems distill'd from poems pass
    away,
The swarms of reflectors and the polite pass, and leave ashes,
Admirers, importers, obedient persons, make but the soil of litera-
    ture,

America justifies itself, give it time, no disguise can deceive it or
    conceal from it, it is impassive enough,
Only toward the likes of itself will it advance to meet them,
If its poets appear it will in due time advance to meet them, there is
    no fear of mistake,
(The proof of a poet shall be sternly deferr'd till his country absorbs
    him as affectionately as he has absorb'd it.)

He masters whose spirit masters, he tastes sweetest who results
    sweetest in the long run,
The blood of the brawn beloved of time is unconstraint;
In the need of songs, philosophy, an appropriate native grand-opera,
    shipcraft, any craft,
He or she is greatest who contributes the greatest original practical
    example.

Already a nonchalant breed, silently emerging, appears on the
    streets,
People's lips salute only doers, lovers, satisfiers, positive knowers,
There will shortly be no more priests, I say their work is done,
Death is without emergencies here, but life is perpetual emergen-
    cies here,
Are your body, days, manners, superb? after death you shall be
    superb,
Justice, health, self-esteem, clear the way with irresistible power;
How dare you place any thing before a man?

14

Fall behind me States!
A man before all—myself, typical, before all.

Give me the pay I have served for,
Give to sing the songs of the great Idea, take all the rest,
I have loved the earth, sun, animals, I have despised riches,
I have given alms to every one that ask'd, stood up for the stupid and
    crazy, devoted my income and labor to others,
Hated tyrants, argued not concerning God, had patience and indul-
    gence toward the people, taken off my hat to nothing known or
    unknown,
Gone freely with powerful uneducated persons and with the young,
    and with the mothers of families,
Read these leaves to myself in the open air, tried them by trees,
    stars, rivers,

Dismiss'd whatever insulted my own soul or defiled my body,
Claim'd nothing to myself which I have not carefully claim'd for
    others on the same terms,
Sped to the camps, and comrades found and accepted from every
    State,
(Upon this breast has many a dying soldier lean'd to breathe his
    last,
This arm, this hand, this voice, have nourish'd, rais'd, restored,
To life recalling many a prostrate form;)
I am willing to wait to be understood by the growth of the taste of
    myself,
Rejecting none, permitting all.

(Say O Mother, have I not to your thought been faithful?
Have I not through life kept you and yours before me?)

15

I swear I begin to see the meaning of these things,
It is not the earth, it is not America who is so great,
It is I who am great or to be great, it is You up there, or any one,
It is to walk rapidly through civilizations, governments, theories,
Through poems, pageants, shows, to form individuals.

Underneath all, individuals,
I swear nothing is good to me now that ignores individuals,
The American compact is altogether with individuals,
The only government is that which makes minute of individuals,
The whole theory of the universe is directed unerringly to one single
    individual—namely to You.

(Mother! with subtle sense severe, with the naked sword in your
    hand,
I saw you at last refuse to treat but directly with individuals.)

16

Underneath all, Nativity,
I swear I will stand by my own nativity, pious or impious so be it;
I swear I am charm'd with nothing except nativity,
Men, women, cities, nations, are only beautiful from nativity.

Underneath all is the Expression of love for men and women,
(I swear I have seen enough of mean and impotent modes of express-
    ing love for men and women,

After this day I take my own modes of expressing love for men and
women.)

I swear I will have each quality of my race in myself,
(Talk as you like, he only suits these States whose manners favor the
audacity and sublime turbulence of the States.)

Underneath the lessons of things, spirits, Nature, governments,
ownerships, I swear I perceive other lessons,
Underneath all to me is myself, to you yourself, (the same monoto-
nous old song.)

17

O I see flashing that this America is only you and me,
Its power, weapons, testimony, are you and me,
Its crimes, lies, thefts, defections, are you and me,
Its Congress is you and me, the officers, capitols, armies, ships, are
you and me,
Its endless gestations of new States are you and me,
The war, (that war so bloody and grim, the war I will henceforth
forget), was you and me,
Natural and artificial are you and me,
Freedom, language, poems, employments, are you and me,
Past, present, future, are you and me.

I dare not shirk any part of myself,
Not any part of America good or bad,
Not to build for that which builds for mankind,
Not to balance ranks, complexions, creeds, and the sexes,
Not to justify science nor the march of equality,
Nor to feed the arrogant blood of the brawn belov'd of time.

I am for those that have never been master'd,
For men and women whose tempers have never been master'd,
For those whom laws, theories, conventions, can never master.

I am for those who walk abreast with the whole earth,
Who inaugurate one to inaugurate all.

I will not be outfaced by irrational things,
I will penetrate what it is in them that is sarcastic upon me,
I will make cities and civilizations defer to me,
This is what I have learnt from America—it is the amount, and it I
teach again.

(Democracy, while weapons were everywhere aim'd at your breast,
I saw you serenely give birth to immortal children, saw in dreams
    your dilating form,
Saw you with spreading mantle covering the world.)

18

I will confront these shows of the day and night,
I will know if I am to be less than they,
I will see if I am not as majestic as they,
I will see if I am not as subtle and real as they,
I will see if I am to be less generous than they,
I will see if I have no meaning, while the houses and ships have
    meaning,
I will see if the fishes and birds are to be enough for themselves, and
    I am not to be enough for myself.

I match my spirit against yours you orbs, growths, mountains,
    brutes,
Copious as you are I absorb you all in myself, and become the master
    myself,
America isolated yet embodying all, what is it finally except myself?
These States, what are they except myself?

I know now why the earth is gross, tantalizing, wicked, it is for my
    sake,
I take you specially to be mine, you terrible, rude forms.

(Mother, bend down, bend close to me your face,
I know not what these plots and wars and deferments are for,
I know not fruition's success, but I know that through war and crime
    your work goes on, and must yet go on.)

19

Thus by blue Ontario's shore,
While the winds fann'd me and the waves came trooping toward me,
I thrill'd with the power's pulsations, and the charm of my theme was
    upon me,
Till the tissues that held me parted their ties upon me.

And I saw the free souls of poets,
 The loftiest bards of past ages strode before me,
Strange large men, long unwaked, undisclosed, were disclosed
    to me.

20

O my rapt verse, my call, mock me not!
Not for the bards of the past, not to invoke them have I launch'd you
    forth,
Not to call even those lofty bards here by Ontario's shores,
Have I sung so capricious and loud my savage song.

Bards for my own land only I invoke,
(For the war, the war is over, the field is clear'd,)
Till they strike up marches henceforth triumphant and onward,
To cheer O Mother your boundless expectant soul.

Bards of the great Idea! bards of the peaceful inventions! (for the
    war, the war is over!)
Yet bards of latent armies, a million soldiers waiting ever-ready,
Bards with songs as from burning coals or the lightning's fork'd
    stripes!
Ample Ohio's, Kanada's bards—bards of California! inland bards—
    bards of the war!
You by my charm I invoke.

1856   1881

Passage to India

1

Singing my days,
Singing the great achievements of the present,
Singing the strong light works of engineers,
Our modern wonders, (the antique ponderous Seven outvied,)
In the Old World the east the Suez canal, *— What is so*
The New by its mighty railroad spann'd, *wonderous about*
The seas inlaid with eloquent gentle wires; *this?*
Yet first to sound, and ever sound, the cry with thee O soul,
The Past! the Past! the Past!

The Past—the dark unfathom'd retrospect!
The teeming gulf—the sleepers and the shadows!
The past—the infinite greatness of the past!
For what is the present after all but a growth out of the past?

(As a projectile form'd, impell'd, passing a certain line, still
    keeps on,
So the present, utterly form'd, impell'd by the past.)

2

Passage O soul to India!
Eclaircise the myths Asiatic, the primitive fables.

Not you alone proud truths of the world,
Nor you alone ye facts of modern science,
But myths and fables of eld, Asia's, Africa's fables,
The far-darting beams of the spirit, the unloos'd dreams,
The deep diving bibles and legends,
The daring plots of the poets, the elder religions;
O you temples fairer than lilies pour'd over by the rising sun!
O you fables spurning the known, eluding the hold of the known,
    mounting to heaven!
You lofty and dazzling towers, pinnacled, red as roses, burnish'd
    with gold!
Towers of fables immortal fashion'd from mortal dreams!
You too I welcome and fully the same as the rest!
You too with joy I sing.

Passage to India!
Lo, soul, seest thou not God's purpose from the first?
The earth to be spann'd, connected by network,
The races, neighbors, to marry and be given in marriage,
The oceans to be cross'd, the distant brought near,
The lands to be welded together.

A worship new I sing,
You captains, voyagers, explorers, yours,
You engineers, you architects, machinists, yours,
You, not for trade or transportation only,
But in God's name, and for thy sake O soul.

3

Passage to India!
Lo soul for thee of tableaus twain,
I see in one the Suez canal initiated, open'd,
I see the procession of steamships, the Empress Eugenie's leading
    the van,

I mark from on deck the strange landscape, the pure sky, the level
    sand in the distance,
I pass swiftly the picturesque groups, the workmen gather'd,
The gigantic dredging machines.

In one again, different, (yet thine, all thine, O soul, the same,)
I see over my own continent the Pacific railroad surmounting every
    barrier,
I see continual trains of cars winding along the Platte carrying
    freight and passengers,
I hear the locomotives rushing and roaring, and the shrill steam-
    whistle,
I hear the echoes reverberate through the grandest scenery in the
    world,
I cross the Laramie plains, I note the rocks in grotesque shapes, the
    buttes,
I see the plentiful larkspur and wild onions, the barren, colorless,
    sage-deserts,
I see in glimpses afar or towering immediately above me the great
    mountains, I see the Wind river and the Wahsatch mountains,
I see the Monument mountain and the Eagle's Nest, I pass the
    Promontory, I ascend the Nevadas,
I scan the noble Elk mountain and wind around its base,
I see the Humboldt range, I thread the valley and cross the river,
I see the clear waters of lake Tahoe, I see forests of majestic pines,
Or crossing the great desert, the alkaline plains, I behold enchant-
    ing mirages of waters and meadows,
Marking through these and after all, in duplicate slender lines,
Bridging the three or four thousand miles of land travel,
Tying the Eastern to the Western sea,
The road between Europe and Asia.

(Ah Genoese thy dream! thy dream!
Centuries after thou art laid in thy grave,
The shore thou foundest verifies thy dream.)

4

Passage to India!
Struggles of many a captain, tales of many a sailor dead,
Over my mood stealing and spreading they come,
Like clouds and cloudlets in the unreach'd sky.

Along all history, down the slopes,
As a rivulet running, sinking now, and now again to the surface rising,

A ceaseless thought, a varied train—lo, soul, to thee, thy sight, they
    rise,
The plans, the voyages again, the expeditions;
Again Vasco de Gama sails forth,
Again the knowledge gain'd, the mariner's compass,
Lands found and nations born, thou born America,
For purpose vast, man's long probation fill'd,
Thou rondure of the world at last accomplish'd.

5

O vast Rondure, swimming in space,
Cover'd all over with visible power and beauty,
Alternate light and day and the teeming spiritual darkness,
Unspeakable high processions of sun and moon and countless stars
    above,
Below, the manifold grass and waters, animals, mountains, trees,
With inscrutable purpose, some hidden prophetic intention,
Now first it seems my thought begins to span thee.

Down from the gardens of Asia descending radiating,
Adam and Eve appear, then their myriad progeny after them,
Wandering, yearning, curious, with restless explorations,
With questionings, baffled, formless, feverish, with never-happy
    hearts,
With that sad incessant refrain, *Wherefore unsatisfied soul?* and
    Whither O mocking life?

Ah who shall soothe these feverish children?
Who justify these restless explorations?
Who speak the secret of impassive earth?
Who bind it to us? what is this separate Nature so unnatural?
What is this earth to our affections? (unloving earth, without a throb
    to answer ours,
Cold earth, the place of graves.)

Yet soul be sure the first intent remains, and shall be carried out,
Perhaps even now the time has arrived.

After the seas are all cross'd, (as they seem already cross'd,)
After the great captains and engineers have accomplish'd their
    work,
After the noble inventors, after the scientists, the chemist, the
    geologist, ethnologist,

[handwritten annotations: "How is this unlike NA?" ; "Mother Earth" ; "Had this happened then or today?"]

Finally shall come the poet worthy that name, *What is Whitman saying here?*
The true son of God shall come singing his songs.

Then not your deeds only O voyagers, O scientists and inventors,
    shall be justified,
All these hearts as of fretted children shall be sooth'd,
All affection shall be fully responded to, the secret shall be told,
All these separations and gaps shall be taken up and hook'd and
    link'd together,
The whole earth, this cold, impassive, voiceless earth, shall be
    completely justified,
Trinitas divine shall be gloriously accomplish'd and compacted by
    the true son of God, the poet,
(He shall indeed pass the straits and conquer the mountains,
He shall double the cape of Good Hope to some purpose,)
Nature and Man shall be disjoin'd and diffused no more,
The true son of God shall absolutely fuse them.

6

Year at whose wide-flung door I sing!
Year of the purpose accomplish'd!
Year of the marriage of continents, climates and oceans!
(No mere doge of Venice now wedding the Adriatic,)
I see O year in you the vast terraqucous globe given and giving all,
Europe to Asia, Africa join'd, and they to the New World,
The lands, geographies, dancing before you, holding a festival
    garland,
As brides and bridegrooms hand in hand.

Passage to India!
Cooling airs from Caucasus, far, soothing cradle of man,
The river Euphrates flowing, the past lit up again.

Lo soul, the retrospect brought forward,
The old, most populous, wealthiest of earth's lands,
The streams of the Indus and the Ganges and their many affluents,
(I my shores of America walking to-day behold, resuming all,)
The tale of Alexander on his warlike marches suddenly dying,
On one side China and on the other side Persia and Arabia,
To the south the great seas and the bay of Bengal,
The flowing literatures, tremendous epics, religions, castes,
Old occult Brahma interminably far back, the tender and junior
    Buddha,

Central and southern empires and all their belongings, possessors,
The wars of Tamerlane, the reign of Aurungzebe,
The traders, rulers, explorers, Moslems, Venetians, Byzantium, the
    Arabs, Portuguese, ~~LARGE CONTRADICTERS~~
The first travelers famous yet, Marco Polo, Batouta the Moor,
Doubts to be solv'd, the map incognita, blanks to be fill'd,
The foot of man unstay'd, the hands never at rest,
Thyself O soul that will not brook a challenge.
~~FOROOT BATTLES US.~~
The mediæval navigators rise before me,
The world of 1492, with its awaken'd enterprise,
Something swelling in humanity now like the sap of the earth in
    spring,
The sunset splendor of chivalry declining.

And who art thou sad shade?
Gigantic, visionary, thyself a visionary,
With majestic limbs and pious beaming eyes,
Spreading around with every look of thine a golden world,
Enhuing it with gorgeous hues.

As the chief histrion,
Down to the footlights walks in some great scena,
Dominating the rest I see the Admiral himself,
(History's type of courage, action, faith,)
Behold him sail from Palos leading his little fleet,
His voyage behold, his return, his great fame,
His misfortunes, calumniators, behold him a prisoner, chain'd,
Behold his dejection, poverty, death.

(Curious in time I stand, noting the efforts of heroes,
Is the deferment long? bitter the slander, poverty, death?
Lies the seed unreck'd for centuries in the ground? lo, to God's due
    occasion,
Uprising in the night, it sprouts, blooms,
And fills the earth with use and beauty.)

7

Passage indeed O soul to primal thought,
Not lands and seas alone, thy own clear freshness,
The young maturity of brood and bloom,
To realms of budding bibles.

O soul, repressless, I with thee and thou with me,
Thy circumnavigation of the world begin,
Of man, the voyage of his mind's return,
To reason's early paradise,
Back, back to wisdom's birth, to innocent intuitions,
Again with fair creation.

8

O we can wait no longer,
We too take ship O soul,
Joyous we too launch out on trackless seas,
Fearless for unknown shores on waves of ecstasy to sail,
Amid the wafting winds, (thou pressing me to thee, I thee to me, O
    soul,)
Caroling free, singing our song of God,
Chanting our chant of pleasant exploration.

With laugh and many a kiss,
(Let others deprecate, let others weep for sin, remorse, humiliation,)
O soul thou pleasest me, I thee.

Ah more than any priest O soul we too believe in God,
But with the mystery of God we dare not dally.

O soul thou pleasest me, I thee,
Sailing these seas or on the hills, or waking in the night,
Thoughts, silent thoughts, of Time and Space and Death, like waters
    flowing,
Bear me indeed as through the regions infinite,
Whose air I breathe, whose ripples hear, lave me all over,
Bathe me O God in thee, mounting to thee,
I and my soul to range in range of thee.

O Thou transcendent,
Nameless, the fibre and the breath,
Light of the light, shedding forth universes, thou centre of them,
Thou mightier centre of the true, the good, the loving,
Thou moral, spiritual fountain—affection's source—thou reservoir,
(O pensive soul of me—O thirst unsatisfied—waitest not there?
Waitest not haply for us somewhere there the Comrade perfect?)
Thou pulse—thou motive of the stars, suns, systems,
That, circling, move in order, safe, harmonious,

Athwart the shapeless vastnesses of space,
How should I think, how breathe a single breath, how speak, if, out
    of myself,
I could not launch, to those, superior universes?

Swiftly I shrivel at the thought of God,
At Nature and its wonders, Time and Space and Death,
But that I, turning, call to thee O soul, thou actual Me,
And lo, thou gently masterest the orbs,
Thou matest Time, smilest content at Death,
And fillest, swellest full the vastnesses of Space.

Greater than stars or suns,
Bounding O soul thou journeyest forth;
What love than thine and ours could wider amplify?
What aspirations, wishes, outvie thine and ours O soul?
What dreams of the ideal? what plans of purity, perfection, strength,
What cheerful willingness for others' sake to give up all?
For others' sake to suffer all?

Reckoning ahead O soul, when thou, the time achiev'd,
The seas all cross'd, weather'd the capes, the voyage done,
Surrounded, copest, frontest God, yieldest, the aim attain'd,
As fill'd with friendship, love complete, the Elder Brother found,
The Younger melts in fondness in his arms.

9

Passage to more than India!
Are thy wings plumed indeed for such far flights?
O soul, voyagest thou indeed on voyages like those?
Disportest thou on waters such as those?
Soundest below the Sanscrit and the Vedas?
Then have thy bent unleash'd.

Passage to you, your shores, ye aged fierce enigmas!
Passage to you, to mastership of you, ye strangling problems!
You, strew'd with the wrecks of skeletons, that, living, never
    reach'd you.

Passage to more than India!
O secret of the earth and sky!
Of you O waters of the sea! O winding creeks and rivers!
Of you O woods and fields! of you strong mountains of my land!
Of you O prairies! of you gray rocks!

O morning red! O clouds! O rain and snows!
O day and night, passage to you!

O sun and moon and all you stars! Sirius and Jupiter! *than Earth*
Passage to you! — *Passage to more*

Passage, immediate passage! the blood burns in my veins!
Away O soul! hoist instantly the anchor!
Cut the hawsers—haul out—shake out every sail!
Have we not stood here like trees in the ground long enough?
Have we not grovel'd here long enough, eating and drinking like
    mere brutes?
Have we not darken'd and dazed ourselves with books long enough?

Sail forth—steer for the deep waters only,
Reckless O soul, exploring, I with thee, and thou with me,
For we are bound where mariner has not yet dared to go,
And we will risk the ship, ourselves and all.

O my brave soul!
O farther farther sail!
O daring joy, but safe! are they not all the seas of God?
O farther, farther, farther sail!

(1868)   1871

Prayer of Columbus

A batter'd, wreck'd old man,
Thrown on this savage shore, far, far from home,
Pent by the sea and dark rebellious brows, twelve dreary months,
Sore, stiff with many toils, sicken'd and nigh to death,
I take my way along the island's edge,
Venting a heavy heart.

I am too full of woe!
Haply I may not live another day;
I cannot rest O God, I cannot eat or drink or sleep,
Till I put forth myself, my prayer, once more to Thee,
Breathe, bathe myself once more in Thee, commune with Thee,
Report myself once more to Thee.

Thou knowest my years entire, my life,
My long and crowded life of active work, not adoration merely;

Thou knowest the prayers and vigils of my youth,
Thou knowest my manhood's solemn and visionary meditations,
Thou knowest how before I commenced I devoted all to come to
  Thee,
Thou knowest I have in age ratified all those vows and strictly kept
  them,
Thou knowest I have not once lost nor faith nor ecstasy in Thee,
In shackles, prison'd, in disgrace, repining not,
Accepting all from Thee, as duly come from Thee.

All my emprises have been fill'd with Thee,
My speculations, plans, begun and carried on in thought of
  Thee,
Sailing the deep or journeying the land for Thee;
Intentions, purports, aspirations mine, leaving results to Thee.

O I am sure they really came from Thee,
The urge, the ardor, the unconquerable will,
The potent, felt, interior command, stronger than words,
A message from the Heavens whispering to me even in sleep,
These sped me on.

By me and these the work so far accomplish'd,
By me earth's elder cloy'd and stifled lands uncloy'd, unloos'd,
By me the hemispheres rounded and tied, the unknown to the
  known.

The end I know not, it is all in Thee,
Or small or great I know not—haply what broad fields, what
  lands,
Haply the brutish measureless human undergrowth I know,
Transplanted there may rise to stature, knowledge worthy Thee,
Haply the swords I know may there indeed be turn'd to reaping-
  tools,
Haply the lifeless cross I know, Europe's dead cross, may bud and
  blossom there.

One effort more, my altar this bleak sand;
That Thou O God my life hast lighted,
With ray of light, steady, ineffable, vouchsafed of Thee,
Light rare untellable, lighting the very light,
Beyond all signs, descriptions, languages;
For that O God, be it my latest word, here on my knees,
Old, poor, and paralyzed, I thank Thee.

My terminus near,
The clouds already closing in upon me,
The voyage balk'd, the course disputed, lost,
I yield my ships to Thee.

My hands, my limbs grow nerveless,
My brain feels rack'd, bewilder'd,
Let the old timbers part, I will not part,
I will cling fast to Thee, O God, though the waves buffet me,
Thee, Thee at least I know.

Is it the prophet's thought I speak, or am I raving?
What do I know of life? what of myself?
I know not even my own work past or present,
Dim ever-shifting guesses of it spread before me,
Of newer better worlds, their mighty parturition,
Mocking, perplexing me.

And these things I see suddenly, what mean they?
As if some miracle, some hand divine unseal'd my eyes,
Shadowy vast shapes smile through the air and sky,
And on the distant waves sail countless ships,
And anthems in new tongues I hear saluting me.
1874   1881

A Noiseless Patient Spider

A noiseless patient spider,
I mark'd where on a little promontory it stood isolated,
Mark'd how to explore the vacant vast surrounding,
It launched forth filament, filament, filament, out of itself,
Ever unreeling them, ever tirelessly speeding them.

And you O my soul where you stand,
Surrounded, detached, in measureless oceans of space,
Ceaselessly musing, venturing, throwing, seeking the spheres to
      connect them,
Till the bridge you will need be form'd, till the ductile anchor
      hold,
Till the gossamer thread you fling catch somewhere, O my soul.
(1862–3)   1881

So Long!

To conclude, I announce what comes after me.

I remember I said before my leaves sprang at all,
I would raise my voice jocund and strong with reference to consum-
mations.

When America does what was promis'd,
When through these States walk a hundred millions of superb per-
sons,
When the rest part away for superb persons and contribute to them,
When breeds of the most perfect mothers denote America,
Then to me and mine our due fruition.

I have press'd through in my own right,
I have sung the body and the soul, war and peace have I sung, and
the songs of life and death,
And the songs of birth, and shown that there are many births.

I have offer'd my style to every one, I have journey'd with confident
step;
While my pleasure is yet at the full I whisper *So long!*
And take the young woman's hand and the young man's hand for the
last time.

I announce natural persons to arise,
I announce justice triumphant,
I announce uncompromising liberty and equality,
I announce the justification of candor and the justification of pride.
I announce that the identity of these States is a single identity only,
I announce the Union more and more compact, indissoluble,
I announce splendors and majesties to make all the previous politics
of the earth insignificant.

I announce adhesiveness, I say it shall be limitless, unloosen'd,
I say you shall yet find the friend you were looking for.

I announce a man or woman coming, perhaps you are the one, (*So
long!*)
I announce the great individual, fluid as Nature, chaste, affection-
ate, compassionate, fully arm'd.

I announce a life that shall be copious, vehement, spiritual, bold,
I announce an end that shall lightly and joyfully meet its translation.

I announce myriads of youths, beautiful, gigantic, sweet-blooded,
I announce a race of splendid and savage old men.

O thicker and faster—(*So long!*)
O crowding too close upon me,
I foresee too much, it means more than I thought,
It appears to me I am dying.

Hasten throat and sound your last,
Salute me—salute the days once more. Peal the old cry once
    more.

Screaming electric, the atmosphere using,
At random glancing, each as I notice absorbing,
Swiftly on, but a little while alighting,
Curious envelop'd messages delivering,
Sparkles hot, seed ethereal down in the dirt dropping,
Myself unknowing, my commission obeying, to question it never
    daring,
To ages and ages yet the growth of the seed leaving,
To troops out of the war arising, they the tasks I have set promulging,
To women certain whispers of myself bequeathing, their affection me
    more clearly explaining,
To young men my problems offering—no dallier I—I the muscle of
    their brains trying,
So I pass, a little time vocal, visible, contrary,
Afterward a melodious echo, passionately bent for, (death making
    me really undying,)
The best of me then when no longer visible, for toward that I have
    been incessantly preparing.

What is there more, that I lag and pause and crouch extended with
    unshut mouth?
Is there a single final farewell?

My songs cease, I abandon them,
From behind the screen where I hid I advance personally solely
    to you.

Camerado, this is no book,
Who touches this touches a man,
(Is it night? are we here together alone?)
It is I you hold and who holds you,
I spring from the pages into your arms—decease calls me forth.

O how your fingers drowse me,
Your breath falls around me like dew, your pulse lulls the tympans of
    my ears,
I feel immerged from head to foot,
Delicious, enough.

Enough O deed impromptu and secret,
Enough O gliding present—enough O summ'd-up past.

Dear friend whoever you are take this kiss,
I give it especially to you, do not forget me,
I feel like one who has done work for the day to retire awhile,
I receive now again of my many translations, from my avataras
    ascending, while others doubtless await me,
An unknown sphere more real than I dream'd, more direct, darts
    awakening rays about me, *So long!*
Remember my words, I may again return,
I love you, I depart from materials,
I am as one disembodied, triumphant, dead.

1860   1881

Alphabetical List of Titles

Alphabetical List of First Lines

16